DEPRESSION AND ANXIETY THERAPY

A BEGINNERS GUIDE TO MASTER YOUR BRAIN AND EMOTIONS. OVERCOME ANXIETY, PANIC ATTACKS, WORRY AND DEPRESSION BY DESTROYING FEAR, PHOBIA AND NEGATIVE THOUGHTS

Table of Contents

Introduction

Depression, which tends to occur more in women than in men, is the direct result of these lingering thoughts. The way it manifests itself can vary depending on a person's age and gender. In men, it may be seen in symptoms such as tiredness, irritability, and sometimes anger. Men tend to behave more recklessly when they are depressed, which can be seen by their abuse of drugs or alcohol. These behaviors may often be passed off as masculine, so they are less likely to recognize it as depression and are not inclined to seek help or treatment.

Women in a depressed state are more likely to appear sad and have deep feelings of worthlessness and guilt. They may be reluctant to take part in social activities or engage with others, even those who are close to them. Depression in children will also be different. Young children may refuse to go to school or show signs of separation anxiety when parents leave. Teenagers are more likely to be irritable, sulky, and often get into trouble in school. In more extreme cases, you might see signs of an eating disorder or substance abuse.

What is anxiety?

Closely associated with depression is anxiety, which can manifest itself in a variety of ways. A mild case of anxiety might be evidenced by the sensation of butterflies in the stomach in anticipation of an important event, concern about meeting deadlines, or nervousness about an anticipated treatment or procedure.

For most people, when anxiety is present, they can just ride it out. It is a normal part of life. However, there are some types of anxiety that are far from the norm. Some anxieties can trigger fears (spiders, snakes, planes, etc.) or phobias that are excessive and irrational fears. Many people have a fear of snakes even though they have never actually come in contact with one. Others are afraid of dogs even though they have never had a bad experience with one. This type of anxiety easily develops into an anxiety disorder.

To help in differentiating between normal anxiety and an anxiety disorder, first take a close look at the cause of the anxiety. Then look at the instinctive response to that fear. If the behavior is considered realistic, then it is probably 'normal' anxiety. However, if the response is viewed as extreme enough to disrupt normal life, it could be classified as an anxiety disorder.

For example, you may be anxious about getting sick, so you take steps to prevent illness. You may use hand sanitizer, regularly wash your hands, or even avoid shaking hands with people in public places. This is a normal form of anxiety. On the other hand, if your fear of getting sick is so strong that you don't want to leave your home or you are constantly washing and cleaning, you may have an anxiety disorder.

There are many different types of anxiety-related disorders out there, and for your convenience, these disorders have been grouped into three different categories:

•   Anxiety disorders

An excessive fear of a real or perceived threat

•   Obsessive-compulsive disorders

Intrusive fearful thoughts that trigger compulsive behaviors

•   Trauma/stressor-related disorders

The extreme reaction to a past traumatic or stress-related event

If you suspect you or someone you know has an anxiety disorder and is struggling to overcome the symptoms, CBT is one way to help. This method of helping patients identify the thought process that triggers the fear may be the best solution to the problem.

How CBT can help

By mastering the techniques in CBT, those with anxiety or depressive disorders can learn how to control those fears and the behaviors they trigger. The program will help to establish clear-cut goals to work on, teach them how to identify the thoughts that start the process, and arm them with defense mechanisms to fight these behaviors.

CBT helps by providing completely new ways to process those thoughts, feelings, and behaviors, so the patients can better cope with these normal events that happen in life. Instead of reacting negatively to traumatic events, it gives them the ability to reframe the triggering event and experience it from an entirely new perspective.

Chapter 1 What Is Anxiety and Depression?

What is the difference between fear and anxiety? Is there a difference between worry and anxiety? How about anxiety and depression? How do things like the stress of emotional feelings of being stressed-out come in? Ever thought of what anger, terror, dread, or nervousness mean and how they relate to anxiety and depression?

What you need to bear in mind is that one of the biggest challenges of working through anxiety is the lack of understanding of what each term means in the first place. One thing you need to realize is that if you are not clear about what it is that you are talking about, then it can be awfully difficult to figure out where it originates from and what to do about it.

So, we will start by defining what these terms mean so that we can understand what anxiety and depression are.

What anxiety is using three levels of experience

If you are going to talk about anything that relates to human psychology - anxiety included – you must distinguish the three major levels of our experiences; physical, emotional, and cognitive.

Physical experience

These refer to sensations that we feel in our bodies. These sensations include; cold, hot, painful, numb, relaxed, moist, tense, achy, dry, and tingly, among others.

Emotional experiences

These are usually the toughest of them all to pin down. The main reason for this is because they are a mix of both cognitive and physical experiences.

Let us consider an instance where you feel anger. In such a situation, you will often find yourself in a state of mind where your thoughts are racing, and you are going through an inner monologue cognitively.

In addition to that, you often begin to experience feelings of hotness, restlessness, and tension. You start to feel as though you are giving up with a combination of images, negative thoughts, and a low-sense of energy, sluggishness, and fatigue, among others. What you need to realize is that emotions are essentially subjective feelings that we experience once we have cognitively interpreted something.

Cognitive experiences

These refer to some form of a mental and intellectual phenomenon or anything else that relates to human thoughts. In most cases, these cognitive experiences are verbal.

For instance, there can be a voice in your head that keeps telling you something about your daily life. It is that inner critic that tries to talk you out of pursuing that dream you have had for years. It keeps narrating to you how you are going to make an epic fail or embarrass yourself in front of everybody.

Thoughts of this nature can also be visual. For instance, you can have that image of your mother when she died on your hands at the hospital or your father when you told them that you were getting married to a man twice your age, or the face of your husband when you asked him for a divorce or those beautiful abs when you lose weight among others.

Events vs. Actions

One thing that is important to bear in mind is that both the physical and cognitive experiences we have defined above can happen to us. It is those times when our tummy grumbles and churns, and the thoughts keep popping into our heads to pick up the groceries on our way home.

These are what we refer to as events.

On the other hand, we often initiate these physical and cognitive experiences directly. For instance, you can choose to wave to your neighbor as they drive past your gate, or working through that problem you have been having in all dimensions right inside your head.

These are what we refer to as actions.

But what about emotional experiences? Well, these are strictly events that happen to us. For instance, when you learn that your loved one has passed away or when you are guilty of treating a friend or family in an awful way, among others. Unlike cognitive experiences, these are not actions that we can initiate directly. The truth is that we cannot just turn off our anger or happiness switch dials.

So, what is the need for these distinctions?

Well, the reason why we need to differentiate between actions and events is that we often get ourselves in all forms of psychological troubles when we assume that our emotions are things we can do or have control over. The tenant of most mental health theories is "we can only indirectly change our emotions" by way of how we choose to think, what we do, or even the surrounding we expose ourselves to.

That said, the next thing is for us to try to see whether we can place anxiety and other related terms within this framework.

Anxiety and other related concepts

Stressors stress and being stressed

These are some of the most common terms used when it comes to anxiety and depression. A stressor refers to anything in your surroundings that is thought of as a threat of challenge. For instance, if you are walking home through woods in your neighborhood, then a tiger starts chasing you, which can be termed as a stressor. If you have an upcoming interview or exam, that too can be a stressor.

One thing that you need to understand is that stress is your body's way of reacting to the presence of a stressor. The stress is often accompanied by the release of adrenaline and the activation of the fight or flight response mechanism.

Some of the most common sensations that come with the response to stress include elevated heart rate, increased blood pressure levels, muscle tension, and rapid breathing, among others. In such an instance, what the brain is trying to do is prepare you so that you are well-positioned to manage the threat, either by fighting or running away.

Being stressed-out, on the other hand, is a term used to describe how we physically feel whenever we are caught in a state of intense stress. What is important to note is that all these events happen on the physical level, even though we often use the term stressed to describe our emotional feelings.

Fear

Fear, on the other hand, is an emotion that often arises as a way of responding to a perceived danger or threat. For instance, when we see a dark shadow or a curly object on a hiking trail, we start to fear because we consider the chance of it being a snake. However, as we draw nearer, we realize that it is just a branch of a tree and that fear goes away, and we keep hiking.

In other words, fear is an emotion that is presence-oriented but lasts for just a short duration of time. It lasts for as long as we still feel a threat within our vicinity. It is also often based on a reasonable assessment of the danger.

Anxiety

Just like fear, anxiety is an emotional feeling that often arises as a result of a response to perceived danger or threat. However, fear is often a response to a realistic threat and subsides soon as the threat disappears. Anxiety, on the other hand, is an emotion that comes as a result of an unrealistic threat.

In other words, your mind imagines something that could happen in the future, no matter how slim that chance of occurrence is. The thing with anxiety is that it tends to persist in intensity and frequency.

Let us consider an instance where you are watching a National Geographic documentary on the most poisonous snakes in the Universe. All of a sudden, you discontinue your hiking plans because you imagine that you could encounter a lethal snake on the trail and get attacked. After this, you start avoiding remote areas of the lake, parks, zoos, and even golf courses. What is even interesting is that you start planning your day to avoid the possibility of encountering a snake.

Panic

Panic, on the other hand, refers to sudden bursts of extreme anxiety that starts within a few minutes and subsides in a couple of minutes, say 15-20 minutes. The thing with panic is that it is often triggered by a catastrophic interpretation of certain signs that are linked to flight and fight responses.

For instance, when your heart starts racing fast, you start thinking that you will have a heart attack. What is important to note is that people who have recurring episodes of panic attacks, it is often triggered by the worry that they could have a panic attack.

Think of panic as anxiety about anxiety!

Terror, Angst, Dread or nervousness

All these are emotional variations of anxiety and fear. Let us take the example of the term dread – this is similar to anxiety except for the fact that it is pervasive and vague. In most instances, it is intense but not as acute because it is somewhat existential.

Worry

Although we use the term worry to explain how we emotionally feel, this term is mostly cognitive. It is often considered as a problem-solving experience that is fast, negative, recurring, and self-assessing. The most interesting thing about worry is that it is not helpful or productive for us in any way.

One thing you need to note is that it is mostly a primary factor that is there to sustain anxiety and stress, causing it to be recurrent.

That said, what you need to takeaway here is that when you are trying to deduce your feelings, you must be as specific as possible. The best framework is for you to determine whether what you are feeling is physical, cognitive, emotional, or a combination of the two or all.

As I already mentioned, emotions are often difficult to define because they are a combination of both physical and cognitive. What is important to note is that emotions are a result of certain interpretations of events that happen to us or our perception.

The most important word here is "interpretation." The point is, there is no way you are going to have emotions without some form of cognitive action happening first. This is a good thing because while we cannot change how we think and interpret the world around us, the cognitive tendencies are long standing habits. This is what forms the basis for cognitive therapy and stoicism.

Chapter 2 How stress and anxiety affect your body and life?

Many of us experience anxiety when we encounter stress-inducing events. In that sense anxiety is a very biological response. But then in some instances, some people experience too much anxiety to the point that it cripples them. Such people are said to have chronic anxiety. When left unchecked, chronic anxiety can be debilitating. But the first and most important step is to recognize that you have this condition. The following signs indicate chronic anxiety in a person.

Extreme Worry

There's nothing wrong with exercising a little caution in your day-to-day life. But if it manifests as a rigid pattern of unfounded worry then there's a problem. Some people have a hard time leading a peaceful existence because of the rigid thoughts of worry going on in their minds. They can run into a simple problem like a tire burst and that is enough to ruin their entire day. People who worry excessively have a tendency to magnify small matters and making them seem like such a big deal. This holds them back from leading a fulfilling life. In order to ascertain that indeed you suffer from extreme worry, you must witness these symptoms for at least six months. Having the tendency of worrying excessively will without a doubt affect you negatively. It causes you to make self-inhibiting decisions and develop a tendency of running away from your issues.

Extreme worry causes you to miss out on many opportunities because you are much too careful and it might turn people away from you.

Agitation

Sufferers of chronic anxiety have a tendency to bulging out of agitation. Their brain may respond to worry by preparing them for a fight. Thus, it diverts resources from various important organs and allocates these resources toward developing rigid muscles. This puts the person in an agitated state. A sufferer of chronic anxiety might seem to be always in a bad mood and as though they are about to get started on a fight.

Thanks to their agitation, such people hurt their chances of integration into society, which usually affects their status in society. Of course, society won't like it if you are the sort of person to threaten other people and to make others feel as though they are walking on eggshells. Also, being easily agitated may put you in many undesirable situations because of threatening other people's egos, which isn't usually a great thing. In worse cases, agitation might cause you to alter your core beliefs, and give room to negative thoughts patterns. If you are the sort of person to become easily agitated you might end up thinking that all human beings are indeed nasty beings and shun people from your life, which will achieve nothing but hurt you in the long run.

Restlessness

A restless person tends to feel as though they are on edge. They cannot concentrate on what they are doing because they are battling against a feeling of being unsettled. Restlessness is particularly common in teens and young adults that are battling chronic anxiety. Teenagers and young adults are especially hard hit with chronic anxiety because they are still in that developmental stage and there are many events to stimulate them. For instance, if they are in college or high school, the social pressure can be immense and cause them to be restless. This restless behavior hinders them from being productive and accomplishing their important life goals.

Additionally, restlessness causes people to take self-inhibiting decisions, and also holds them back from thinking through their decisions, which can have a negative effect on the quality of their lives. When someone feels restless, they tend to want to isolate themselves, which can gradually invite loneliness into their lives. But then again, not every sufferer of chronic anxiety will struggle with restlessness.

Exhaustion

In as much as anxiety is associated with extra-arousal and hyperactivity, some victims tend to experience exhaustion as well. The link between exhaustion and anxiety is largely down to the victim's personality. For instance, if a person is an introvert, they will process their chronic anxiety by thinking about it extensively, which is a resource-intensive exercise. Thinking about stuff that bothers you for an extended amount of time can cause you to deplete your energy, thus developing exhaustion. Also, when chronic anxiety leads to issues like insomnia or muscle tension, they will take a toll on an individual's energy reserve, and cause them to battle with low energy levels. Once exhaustion kicks in as a result of the individual's struggle against anxiety, it can affect their life in a myriad of ways. For one, it keeps them from being productive, and by extension, it can hurt their wellbeing. Exhaustion might also cause a person to develop a self-inhibiting mentality as they are in doubt of their potential.

In the long run, this condition might keep one from reaching their important life goals, because they are at risk of losing their motivations.

Lack of Focus

Studies reveal that one of the first casualties of chronic anxiety is focus. Most people who are battling chronic anxiety can hardly concentrate on the tasks before them.

This explains why students who battle anxiety have a hard time performing in class. Before you can accomplish any endeavor, your mind ought to be operating from a relaxed point, else you will lose the energy to focus on your important life goals. Without focus, it doesn't matter that you are skilled or resourceful, but you are likely to fail short of your goals. This is because anything worth achieving takes hard work, which promotes the skill of concentration. Once you begin experiencing anxiety, your brain gives that matter huge importance, and it denies the concentration so that you might first address the root cause of your anxiety. Most people struggle to keep their focus afloat against the judgment of their brain and this usually leads them to become extremely conflicted. It is only logical to first address the anxiety issues and then your brain will become supportive in increasing the skill of focus.

Irritability

In more than 90% of cases, people with chronic anxiety tend to be irritable. It would be hard for an extremely anxious person to keep a calm attitude. Their anxiety causes them to feel as though the world is conspiring to hurt them. This causes them to keep their guards up. Anxious people tend to be extra sensitive to words and nuances and they go deeper than everyone else in trying to glean meaning. What might sound normal to the average person might be offensive to the anxious person, thanks to their tendency to think hard on matters, reading cues that had not been implied. Irritability is one trait that holds people back from experiencing fulfillment. And this is down to the fact that it antagonizes people. An irritable person is likely to have many enemies and develop a bad reputation in society. Being irritable can frustrate many aspects of the victim's life, and eventually cause them to develop a negative attitude toward other human beings.

Muscle tension

Another outcome of chronic anxiety is the development of tense muscles.

 Of course, not everyone battling muscle tension suffers from chronic anxiety. But the explanation is that the excessive worry attributed to anxiety causes the body to experience difficulties in normal functioning. Thus, the tendons become stiff and result in muscle tension. What's interesting is the fact that the treatment of muscle tension through various relaxation exercises tones down the anxiety. Chronic anxiety tends to have an adverse effect on more than one area of an individual's life. With sore muscles, the individual is discouraged from moving about, which is an ambitious move on the brain's part to make the person face his problem. Muscle tension denies the victim the peace of mind to function in a normal capacity. They find themselves having to rely on external support, and if the circumstances prolong, it can be incredibly underwhelming.

Insomnia

This is a common sign of chronic anxiety. There's a strong link between chronic anxiety and an inability to sleep. For one, the excessive worrying puts the mind on overdrive and this denies the victim the chance to fall asleep. Also, chronic anxiety might meddle with an individual's physiological makeup and result in lack of sleep. But this situation puts the victim at a huge disadvantage considering that sleep plays a huge role in an individual's wellbeing. One of the main ways that lack of sleep affects an individual is by lowering their productivity.

Assuming your job demands watchfulness, like a driver or a plant operator, you would not be in a position to deliver great results, since your lack of sleep would get in the way.

Lack of sleep would affect your cognitive abilities. This results in you being unable to reach the summit in regards to your potential. Extensive sleep loss can affect your capacity to partake tasks that demand sharp critical thinking capacity. In the long run, subpar performance may affect your capacity to build a good reputation in your line of work.

Lack of sleep would be a gateway to a host of other health complications such as heart failure, high blood pressure, stroke, and diabetes. One of the major problems of chronic anxiety is that it triggers a compounding effect on your failing health. Loss of sleep, which is born of anxiety, causes the development of illnesses, which end up scramming off whatever little health you had.

Thus, it is critical to get rid of chronic anxiety as fast as one can.

Panic attacks

Depending on your life experiences, panic attacks are to a certain extent quite normal. But then if you experience overwhelming fear on a daily basis that's a sign you have chronic anxiety. Panic attacks manifest as intense episodes of fear that shake the person to their core and leave them fearing for their life.

They are characterized by things such as rapid heartbeat, shortness of breath, and sweating. The triggers behind panic attacks may vary, but victims experience the same intense dread.

One of the effects of panic attacks is social withdrawal. Someone who's been experiencing panic attacks is wont to withdraw from society and construct their own little world, scared of everybody else. Sadly, such an attitude only worsens their situation and makes it hard for them to live productively.

People with panic attacks have a tendency to shun everyone from their lives. They seem to not trust anyone and this hinders them from forming rewarding relationships. In the long run, such a mentality causes them to develop a negative attitude toward human beings in general.

In worst-case scenarios, panic attacks can lead someone to commit suicide. Considering that panic attacks overwhelm the person with fear and cause them to feel as though they are about to die, the victim might think it okay to just end their life and get it over with.

Avoiding social arrangements

Considering that human beings are social animals, and our survival depends on our collaborative efforts, then being a little cautious about how others perceive you is quite normal. But when we talk about someone suffering from chronic anxiety, we are talking of someone that actively avoids any form of social interaction. When they meet someone, they tend to be extremely shy and then afterward they judge themselves harshly.

It is extremely disadvantageous on the part of the victim for them to pull away from people because they deny themselves the chance to fulfill some important goals which can only be fulfilled in a social context.

If they must take part in an upcoming social event, the victim will be consumed with worry, wondering whether or not people will take a liking to them, which can be incredibly limiting. Their worst fear is to be embarrassed in front of other people.

The number of affected Americans is steadily growing, and it seems in the not-so-far future, people will have an especially hard time socializing.

Phobias

Another huge sign of chronic anxiety is the presence of phobias. These fears have no logical roots. The victim develops an irrational dread against certain things or events. And once their fear is triggered, it stops them from functioning normally. Some of the phobias that people develop include:

1. Animal phobias

2. Environmental phobias

3. Certain situation phobias

4. Injury-related phobias

Indigestion

Another huge indication of chronic anxiety is an inability to digest food. The victim's brain usually channels most of the resources toward getting rid of anxiety, but this impairs the body's ability to digest food in a normal way, resulting in abdominal discomfort. Of course, one may develop for reasons other than chronic anxiety e.g. eating/drinking too much, being intolerant to certain foods, and swallowing pills when hungry. But in order to ascertain that your indigestion is as a result of chronic anxiety look at the accompanying symptoms.

Stomach complications tend to hold one back from leading a productive life as the abdominal discomfort is too much to handle. In extreme cases, they can open one up to various illnesses that affect the functioning of various organs.

Compulsive habits

Usually, when an individual is battling chronic anxiety, there'll be something that they obsess about. They cannot go for long without indulging their need to satiate this compulsive urge. Of course, this is a stressful condition to have. For instance, if the victim holds some anxiety about the pimples on their face, they might post a photo of their face on social media, hoping to be reassured that their face is all right, and then check every two minutes whether people have replied by liking or commenting. They hope to gain validation from other people, and they are incredibly sensitive to criticism. Of course, such tendencies are extremely crippling. The world is a harsh battleground and softies tend to have a rough time. Unless one learns to accept – and be proud of – who they are, then they are going to have a hard time reaching their important life goals.

Perfectionism

In a conventional sense, perfectionists look like ambitious people who will rest at nothing to ensure that whatever they envisioned comes to life. But then psychology tells us that chronic anxiety is sometimes the force behind perfectionism. It makes perfect sense that if someone cares too much about a particular result, they might develop a tendency to be attached to the creation process, which will see them take extra caution and act meticulously. Steve Jobs, the late co-founder of Apple Inc., is a prime example of a perfectionist. He was so involved in the creation process of his company's products and he would make employees do tasks over and over again until he reached his goal just as he'd envisioned it. Obviously, people considered him to be ambitious, but the people that were close to him revealed that he was indeed an anxious man. But sometimes perfectionism might be born of something else other than chronic anxiety.

Chapter 3 Self-help Exercises for Anxiety

Depression doesn't have to get the best of you or control your life. It does require you to take a few important steps to get ahead of the challenges it presents. To begin, seek professional counsel. You can speak with friends and family for support but only a professional can diagnose and treat you properly. In addition to professional care, you should be proactive in your coping techniques. Not everyone will respond the same to self-help, but the following could help decrease or alleviate symptoms that may appear.

Tips for Dealing with Depression

In addition, these steps are iatrical in providing you the needed strength to manage daily living and to eliminate factors that place your mental well-being at risk.

Physical Activities

Physical activity gives your body the strength it needs to sustain from day to day. Research indicates that physical activities ignite positive chemicals that works to enhance mood.

There are several available methods to stay or introduce activity into your lifestyle. Regardless of your physical state or desire, finding exercises to incorporate into your day to day can be enjoyable and useful. Consider activities such as yoga, Zumba, running, swimming or cycling. If you desire or require something easier, consider walking or jogging at a slow pace. You can incorporate exercise into your daily routine by parking farther away from the entrance, walking the dog to the park that's further away from home or walking to the shopping center or work.

Try to incorporate at least one to two hours of physical activity per week. Keep track of activities that elevate your heart rate and engage all the muscles of the body.

Eat Well

Eating a healthy and well-balanced diet is important at all times, but especially when coping with depression. The energy obtained from food serves as fuel for your mental and physical state.

It is common for most to intake three meals and one to two light snacks per day. A healthy diet consists of lean proteins, fresh veggies and fruits, whole grains and low-fat dairy. The consumption of healthy and nutritious foods makes you feel great throughout the day. Avoid pre-packaged foods when possible and consider gardening when possible to keep fresh foods nearby and easily accessible.

You need to hydrate by drinking sufficient amounts of water. It's easy to determine how much water you should take in.

Simply divide your weight by two and drink that amount in ounces each day.

Rest Well

A good night's rest is an essential element in leading a healthy and fulfilled life. Sleep recharges the body and helps it to prepare for the next day. The brain begins to feel cluttered and fatigued without efficient amounts of sleep. Eight to ten hours each night is the suggested amount for teenagers. Most adults can thrive on seven to eight hours of sleep each night. It may be challenging to get the necessary amount of sleep, especially when depressed.

Begin by making the area you sleep in relaxing. Try falling asleep in a cool room with dim or dark lights. You may need to add blinds or shades to the window to decrease light interference. Consider sleeping with ear plugs, a fan and comfortable pillows and bedding. The hour prior to retiring for the night should be a relaxed one. Put down the phone, homework or work that you brought home from the office. Drink water if thirsty and avoid caffeine within that hour also. Avoid spicy foods and sugary snacks.

Wondering what can help you unwind if you have to say no to all your feel-good things? Take a soak in the tub or warm shower. Read your favorite novel or motivational guide. Sip on warm tea or milk and listen to soft music before bed. These are great ways to prepare your body mentally and physically for a good night's rest.

Address Any Issues with Your Health

Your emotional state improves when you tackle health issues head-on. You feel better because you've taken the initiative to take care of yourself. Many people who live with unaddressed health issues worry endlessly about what could be wrong or what may happen. Research indicates that there is an association between unaddressed health issues and feelings of depression, specifically inflammatory ailments. Taking care of health concerns could work to enhance your mood because you're not dealing with constant pain and other illnesses.

Stay Away from Unsafe Substances

Coping with stress is never easy. There are positive and negative ways to deal with factors that lead to stress. A negative approach includes taking part in activities that may enhance your mood at the moment but will eventually leave you feeling down. These activities include but aren't limited to the use of illegal drugs, abuse of alcohol and exhibiting dangerous behaviors such as cutting or huffing.

Exist in the Moment

Stay in tune with your mind and inner peace. When overwhelm sets in, it's easy to focus on past issues or things that are going on in the background. These thoughts can cause feelings of depression and unjust stress. Existing in the moment encourages you to free your mind of anything negative, which helps you to concentrate on your happiness in that moment. This existence should take place when you are with friends, family or alone.

Practice S.I.T.E.

Before your day begins, at the climax of your day, while traveling home, in the shower or before falling asleep, initiate F.I.T.E.

Freeze and stop doing whatever you're doing for a moment.

Inhale. Breathe as usual and take natural breaths in and out the nose.

Think clearly. Actually, ponder your thoughts. Assess what they mean. Acknowledge and accept whatever you observe. Focus on your mind, body and any physical perceptions you experience during this time. Notice if your heart races, muscles tighten or pain sets in.

Exercise anything that supports you at this very moment. It may be speaking with family or friends or stretching before bed.

Proceed with Love

This may sound easy but most people coping with depression find it extremely difficult. The requirements of school, work and family can make it difficult to approach or do the things we actually love to do. Engage in activities that enhance your life. Paint, dance, volunteer or bake a cake. Whatever brings you joy, do it!

Tips to Help You Cope with Depression

You should work to discover ways to help you cope with depression. This is a powerful coping mechanism that assists you in working through the daily spurts of feeling down and overwhelmed. There are effective ways to cope with emotional, mental and physical setbacks. One extremely effective approach is exercise because it gets you up and moving. It is also a beneficial tool in helping to clear your mind of random or oppressive thoughts.

Elevated mood is one of the most impactful strategies or techniques utilized to cope with disorders such as anxiety. You may consider adopting a regular exercise regimen, scheduling a weekly connect with a current or old friend or taking a class to learn something new. These are merely ideas that may work in getting you through the coping process. Effective coping helps you to remove the fog that clouds your mind, judgement and feelings. It results in a happy and extremely outgoing lifestyle that makes each day worth celebrating.

Below are additional strategies or suggestions to help cope with depression.

Don't Abandon Your Support System

Depression will make you feel that you have no one around who is willing to help. This is common when dealing with low self-esteem. While your days may be spent in isolation and feeling lonely, you are not alone. There are friends and family who want you to be happy again. It is challenging to battle depression alone. You likely feel ashamed or embarrassed about neglecting friends or family, but you should put these feelings to rest. Connect with your social circle and family to enhance your mood. This will do wonders for you. You will discover that communicating with those who care about you and your well-being instills a sense of renewed strength within you.

If you feel alone and think there is no one to lean on, establish new relationships to strengthen your bridge of support.

Utilizing these suggestions may help you to stay connected.

• Seek support from those who encourage you to be who you truly are. The goal isn't to find someone who can make you better. You just need someone who will lend a listening ear. This person should be understanding, compassionate and sensitive to what you're feeling.

• Arrange a face –to-face. It's always a great idea to text or get a phone call but nothing is better than face-to-face interaction. Facial expressions are iatrical in expressing and understanding the struggles or challenges a person is facing.

Talk it over and feel relief in no time because you have connected with someone who cares about your issues.

• Mend your social butterfly wing. At one time you were the social butterfly, but depression has caused one of your wings to become damaged. Get out and mingle, even when your mind and body is telling you not to do so. It helps to associate with others in that it puts your mind on positive things and helps to relieve your feelings of depression.

• Be someone's support system. You like to feel supported and should offer that same support to others. This is a great mood enhancer in that it helps you to feel good about yourself when helping others. Listen to someone else's problem or volunteer to help the less fortunate. You feel different when you know that what you're doing or who you are is making a difference.

• Find a support channel. It may be helpful to speak with others who are dealing with depression. It helps you to feel less isolated and presents an opportunity for you to be encouraged and offer encouragement to others.

Tips to Stay in Touch with Your Support Outlet

• Choose at least one person to discuss what you're going through

• Help others with their issues

- Meet a friend for coffee or a movie

- Have a friend or co-worker check in on you occasionally

- Join someone for a social outing

- Reach out to an old friend

- Choose a workout partner

- Arrange weekly lunch or dinner outings

- Join a class to see new faces

- Speak with a counselor, clergy or therapist

Reconnect with Things You Enjoy

To effectively battle depression, you must reconnect with enjoyable things and make you feel energized. Examples include practicing healthy living, effectively managing overwhelming situations, doing only the things you feel you can achieve and adding enjoyable activities to your daily routine.

Do Something You Enjoy. Although it may be challenging to do so while feeling depressed, you must motivate yourself to do something you enjoy or at one time found exciting to do. Getting up and going out to do your favorite things can make you feel happy and accomplished. It may not be an immediate relief to your depression, but it will help to capitalize on our positive feelings at the moment. Revisit an old hobby or activity you once enjoyed. Connect with your creative side by engaging in music, dance, art or theater. Visit a park or museum.

Become Health Conscious. Become aware of your health by first, getting enough rest. If depression is an issue, chances are, you're losing or getting too much sleep. Adapt a health schedule that enables a rejuvenated feeling when you awake.

Alleviate stress wherever possible. Stress is a primary contributor to depression. It acts as a trigger and causes it to become worse over time. Identify the elements in your life that trigger your stress meter and define ways to eliminate it and get a grasp on your life.

Calming Techniques. Practice techniques or strategies that help you to feel relaxed. Relaxation is a key tool to relieving and eliminating stress and depression. Suggestions for calming exercises include meditation, muscle engagement and yoga.

Here is a "happiness toolkit" to help you battle depression.

- Get out and embrace nature

- Make a list of things you love about yourself

- Choose a book to read each month

- Enjoy a funny sitcom or movie

- Enjoy a nice warm bubble bath

- Tackle a few small chores

- Visit or volunteer at the animal shelter

- Talk with friends in person

- Turn up the music and dance

- Make a spontaneous decision to do something different

Move Around

As simple as it sounds, people living with depression find it extremely difficult to just move around. Getting out of bed, exiting the vehicle, getting out of their own way, and getting out of the house is simply hard to accomplish when depressed. Adopting an active lifestyle is a critical weapon in the fight against depression. According to research, exercise is equally beneficial in dealing with depression as medication may be. Commit to participate in exercise or some type of physical activity for at least half-an-hour per day. You can break the time up into increments or do it all at once. Just figure out how to be more active each day.

Exercise is a Mood Enhancer

You will feel less fatigued. In the beginning it may be hard but eventually, your fatigue will become less with exercise or physical activity. Increased energy levels are primary mood enhancers.

Stay in rhythm. Participate in exercises or activities that are consistent and rhythmic, as they are great for battling depression. Consider walking, dancing, weight class or swimming, as these all engage both the upper and lower extremities.

Engage your feelings. If you are depressed because of a traumatic experience, get in touch with how your body responds or reacts to movement. Notice the little things like the moment your foot touches the ground, how lightly the wind hits your cheek or your breathing patterns.

Get Sun-Kissed

Sunlight delivers a healthy dose of Vitamin D, and the D is not for depression. Sunshine helps to elevate levels of serotonin, which stimulates the mood. Take in 15-20 minutes of sunlight each day. Use sunscreen when necessary and never gaze directly into the sunlight.

Here are ways to connect with sunlight.

•	Enjoy a lunchtime walk, sip your coffee on the deck or eat lunch on the patio

•	Get moving outside instead of in a gym or in front of the television. Play tennis or hike a trail to enjoy nature while soaking in the sun.

•	Allow more natural sunlight inside your house by raising the blinds or peeling back the drapes of the windows.

- If sunshine is not frequent in your area, consider light therapy techniques or boxes

Combat Negative Thoughts

Are you feeling day after day feeling vulnerable or powerless? Are you thinking that you're in a hopeless situation and there's nothing you can do to change it? Depression has the tendency to creep into your mind and make every thought you generate a negative one. You begin to think negatively about yourself and everything you encounter.

These negative thought associations are not okay. Don't allow them to manipulate or overwhelm your existence. It won't be easy to terminate the negative thoughts, but it is possible. Each time a negative thought enters your mind, extinguish it with a positive twist to the thought. You'll be creating a balance in your thought process and alleviating in negativity that exists.

Negative Thoughts That Give Depression Power Over Your Life

Establish a middle ground. Your thought process doesn't have to be all or nothing. You don't have to get every answer correct and there is room for error in every decision you make. Acknowledge this and be okay with it.

One negative result doesn't defy the person you really are. Don't allow a single idea or action that went wrong in your life to define you. It's no indication that everything else will fail. More importantly, it doesn't make you a failure.

Erase the negative over positive mentality. Depression will make you overlook every positive thing that goes right in your life and cause you to focus only on the negative. Think of all the good and positive things that happen to you. These will by far outweigh the negative.

Stop drawing conclusions without proof or facts. You are ruining your life by always assuming you can predict the outcome of things. You have no idea the length of time it will take you to finish school. The point is that you must begin somewhere. It doesn't matter how long it takes you as long as you finish.

Emotional nonsense. Your feelings of defeat or failure are nonsense. You spend day after day telling yourself that you are a failure or not good at anything. You are the only person that feels this way and without reason, it's only your depressed emotions that make you think so.

The "I Can't" syndrome. Stop telling yourself that you can't do something that you've not attempted. The category of your desired things to do is the starting list of things that can be done if you are proactive in making them happen.

Get Out of the Box. You cannot remain isolated or enclosed inside a box because of past mistakes. Stop calling yourself a failure or worthless. You're neither of those things.

Give Your Negative Connotations the Third-Degree

Once the negative thought patterns that live inside your head have been identified, it's time to bring them in for questioning. Ask yourself:

• What facts or proof make this, or these thoughts have substance? No substance?

• What would I advise a loved one or friend who thought this way?

• Can I look at this from another perspective or is there another reason that this has happened?

• How would I view this if depression weren't involved?

Chapter 4 Physical Activity

So now that you have found the motivation to begin to go your workout routine. Onto the difficult part - how do you begin on an exercise?

When you are mentally healthy and a fitness freak, then chances are you hardly think about your actions in the gym. Hell, they could just be motions that you are going through since you have reached the point where your brain no longer thinks through what you are doing because of the conditioned reflex.

Once you drop your gym bag, you move forward and only regain your senses when you are in the shower at the end of it all.

But being depressed or anxious puts some perspective into your actions. When your mind is in a constant state of worry about you and the world and how it reacts to you, you scrutinize every action. Even when you are a fitness freak and develop depression or anxiety, that breaks your cycle. Suddenly, you lack the desire to go to the gym. You self-doubt a lot more than usual.

If you aren't a fitness freak, you will hardly want anything to do with doing more than just shuffling around the bed. Yet, once you break through the barrier and find the propulsion to move to the next step, the beginning is a tedious process. Whatever you see ahead of you becomes something huge and marvelous, and not in an interesting way. You suddenly wish to crawl back to bed. But should you? No, let's look at ways you can start.

Take Small Steps

One of the worst things about depression and anxiety is that they often have the ability to make routine tasks seem like insurmountable behemoths that will crush you under their weight if you dare lift a finger towards them.

So, the best way to get around this is to break down the task into small parts, or if not, then to begin taking small steps.

If you have decided to join the gym, rather than go straight to working out, you could begin by doing some basic exercises in your house.

If you intend to walk and find it hard to get out of the house, begin walking around your house.

Have an Idea of the Result

Create a vision of how you would want the end of your workout to be. When you have the end in mind, what this helps do is then remove the doubts and anxiety that would come with being uncertain; thus, you will better be able to come up with a plan on how you want to go about your routine.

This will also be key in helping you keep the motivation. Since you have an idea of the end result, you will always have that in mind when the depression or anxiety becomes too crippling.

Write Down Your Routine

When you do this, keep in mind that while you would want something that will challenge you and push you, having a routine that is too ambitious will have the opposite effect to what you are aiming for.

When you wake up each morning, go through what you have written down and try to identify what you would easily accomplish throughout the day. From here on, this will help you find the motivation you need to build a consistent way of doing things when it comes to exercising.

And once you have done something, and feel like it no longer offers you the challenge you want, cancel it out.

Create a Stimuli

A stimulus is something that makes you take action.

When you are depressed or anxious, you will most certainly need more than just motivation. You will need to cultivate something that will provide you with a reminder of what you are meant to do - in this case, start that exercise.

This could be something as small as putting your work-out apparatus next to the bed so that they are the first thing you see in the morning. If you workout in the evening, you could put them somewhere close to the door, a place where you will easily see when you get into your house.

You could also put a reminder on your phone that will provide you with cues to begin your exercise.

If you work out with friends, you can agree to be calling each other the day before the exercise and again, on the day of the exercise so as to see each other through the routine.

Don't Be Afraid of Lauding Yourself

When you find it within you to get out of bed and begin with your routine, this is something that is worth celebrating.

When you are deep in the agonizing grasps of depression or anxiety, or a potent combination of both, which is not uncommon, getting the strength to just leave your bed is an effort that you should take in your stride.

When you are trying to live positively with depression or anxiety, one of the most important pieces of advice you will often get is that every action you take towards getting yourself to be better is a step in the right direction. So, when you make the smallest efforts with the biggest intentions, celebrate it.

When you find yourself in the situation where you are able to make concerted efforts towards joining an exercise group, this is a major leap. When you find yourself contemplating joining the gym, or doing exercises even when you have that niggling feeling that you don't want to, that is courage. You are moving well against the desires of your depression or anxiety, and this is something that you should take pride in.

So, for every push against your depression or anxiety, give yourself credit. Getting by well with mental health is one of the hardest things one can do. So, if you find yourself able to carry through the day when you are able to will yourself into getting into the right mindset to get on with exercise, something that even those in proper mental health struggle to stay true to, make a point of congratulating yourself.

Even as you do this though, remember that once you get into the groove of doing something, you should be able to do it even when you feel terrible. Getting going should be at the top of your mind before getting going perfectly. Making that first step is important. Make it count each time and you will find yourself making progress.

Take Time Out

Take a rest when you feel like it. Chances are when you are coming out of a bout of depression or anxiety; you will often have limited energy. So, when you begin your workout and feel tired shortly after, don't hesitate to put on the brakes and cool your heels. It is worth it and will help improve your desire.

Frequent breaks in your workout routine could also help you get lost in your thoughts if at all the workout isn't getting you in your groove.

The steps listed above are simple but effective ways in which you should follow to give yourself great chances of being able to understand and deal with your depression. It is important that you are able to practice the above according to how they impact you. If you put too much pressure on yourself to get through all the processes, the results could be counterproductive.

Dealing with depression requires a delicate balance even as you pull yourself through with willpower. Therefore, make a point of doing it well.

Chapter 5 Nature Therapy

Nature therapy, also known as ecotherapy, has been gaining popularity over the years. Not only have nature enthusiasts embraced these techniques as a way of improving their mental health, but reputable scientists have even taken interest in studying the positive effects of nature on the human brain. Human beings came from nature and so it makes sense that spending all of our time cooped up indoors without much exposure to sunlight can have negative effects on our brains. And, according to science, there's more to it than just vitamin D.

Aside from obtaining better mental health, the many ways in which nature can help you improve your life include gaining better physical health, gaining new skills associated with being outdoors, and connecting with mother nature. Going outside on a regular basis also helps motivate you to stay active and stick with your exercise routines, particularly if those routines are done outside. And, to top it off, if you include other people in your outdoors activities, this can lead to a more active social life, which has also been attributed to better moods.

Physical health benefits of nature therapy include healthier levels of vitamin D, weight loss, and it can actually improve the functioning of your brain. This goes far beyond the mood boosting effects of nature and sunlight. Many people who spend time outdoors report having a better clarity of thought afterwards.

One scientific study by the Stanford Woods Institute for the Environment revealed that spending an hour and a half walking in a natural setting, surrounded by nature and away from city areas, caused a decreased level of activity in a specific part of the brain that has been associated with depression. Could our urbanized lifestyles be linked to increasing rates of depression? Many people believe this might be so.

There are established programs and ecotherapists available around the world to guide you through green therapy and they're all great, but this book is written for people who want to get started all by themselves or with a group of close individuals looking to improve their mental health by using the power of mother nature.

Nature therapy involves a wide selection of treatment options that use mother nature to alleviate symptoms of depression. These options include going on outdoors adventures, gardening, outdoors exercises, outdoors craft projects, spending time in the wilderness, and so much more. Throughout this book, we'll take a look at these and various other ways that you can use mother nature to help you beat depression.

See the last page of this book for a list of resources that can help people suffering from depression.

Chapter 6 Beginning Mantra Meditation

A term you may have heard about in relation to CBT is "Mindfulness." So, what is it? Developed for individuals who suffer from frequent, recurring, and often severe depressions, Mindfulness combines CBT techniques with breathing exercises, meditation, visualization, and other such techniques that can empower one to move past stress and back into more productive modes of thinking.

Basic Principles

Mindfulness requires you to stop ruminating in the past and worrying about the future. When you are feeling anxious, you know that you can't just stop. When it comes to Mindfulness, the aim is to help you reduce your momentary anxiety by grounding you in the present moment.

Mindfulness techniques are methods to pull your thoughts from the rumination over past events you can no longer control. Whenever you are thinking of something embarrassing that happened, or maybe an event that you are worried will sneak back up on you, it can keep you from enjoying the moment.

Similarly, if you are always stressed about the future, then you will start to lose yourself in the present moment, and sometimes other people will notice that you are not all there. Thinking about the future doesn't always involve negative thoughts. You may fantasize about a life that's seemingly unachievable, one with fancy houses, money, and more friends and family to provide comfort. Though these thoughts don't necessarily cause anxiety, they can lead to depression when avoiding current problems by fantasizing about a future that may never come.

Mindfulness involves any activity that is going to pull you from these moments and bring you to the present—a time that matters most. These types of fantasies and rumination patterns are forms of dissociation.

Disassociation can be debilitating. You may find yourself so stuck in bed that you can't move. Other times, it can affect your memory.

How Mindfulness is Connected to CBT

Since CBT is about rewiring your brain, Mindfulness will help give you a way to stop unrealistic fantasies before they get started. Instead of giving into a thought, a Mindfulness technique will help you bring yourself back to the present.

Sometimes one starts to disassociate because they don't want to confront a certain issue. If you are triggered by something or someone, you might mentally remove yourself from the situation and think of something else. This adjustment in thought may help temporarily, but you are still not managing your root issues. You should know how to use CBT Mindfulness techniques to better prepare you for these attempts at disassociation.

How Mindfulness Can Help

Have you ever sat through a class and thought, "I need to pay attention.I need to focus." Then, an hour later, the class has ended, and you realize you fantasized about what you were going to do over the weekend or maybe pictured yourself on a trip in a tropical area. Instead of paying attention to class, your mind was in a different state, so when you attempt to study, it is more challenging than it would have been if you had paid attention.

Mindfulness will help pull you back to the classroom. Sometimes we know what it takes to pay attention, but we don't always catch ourselves when we start daydreaming. You don't always recognize that you are disassociating until after the fact when you ask yourself where you are or what happened in the past few minutes. When we disassociate too often, negative side effects will emerge including anxiety, confusion, and memory loss.

Mindfulness

Mindfulness is similar to meditation, but it doesn't have to be practiced in the same way. You can be mindful while standing behind the cash register at work. Mindfulness can be practiced when you are in the middle of a conversation with a friend. You can even be mindful when you are on the couch alone in your house. There are many chances for someone to be mindful, and there are no set rules of when and where you can practice it. It is all up to you and the situation in which you are trying to be mindful.

There are different ways of being mindful, but as you practice more, you should come up with a method of your own. Not everyone is going to find that each of these methods works for them, so make sure you select what is most appropriate for you. These methods can be done when you are sitting on your couch and stressing over something that is out of your control. Or, if you are trying to fall asleep and the depressive thoughts won't stop, be mindful.

Furthermore, when you are at a party and you are worried about how you look or what you are saying to others, be mindful. When you see something that is triggering but you can't leave the situation, be mindful. Basically, whenever you feel like you need more than what is available to you, it is a good idea to practice Mindfulness. It can seem scary and overwhelming, but it is up to you to do your best to keep yourself grounded in reality and not in your invasive, intruding, distorted, and unhealthy thoughts.

Remember when going through these exercises that if your mind happens to drift back to anxious thoughts, don't punish yourself. Just do your best to keep redirecting your mind to the present. It will be challenging at first.

The more you practice these methods, however, the easier it will be to stay connected to the present and not drift off into the future or stay stuck in the past. You will have a better sense of how to keep thinking about the "now" rather than anything else that is causing you anxiety.

Group Mindfulness is important as well. If you work in a business setting with many other people, then you know that you can sometimes pick up on their stress, causing your own to heighten. If Mindfulness is practiced in groups, it will help everyone's health overall.

Games are a great way to be mindful. Look into free phone games you can play that will help you reduce stress. Whenever you are feeling anxious, you can play the game rather than sit with your anxious thoughts. In a group setting or in an individual sense, puzzles are also great ways to help keep you mindful. You might consider putting one on a table at a party to help keep people distracted when things aren't as active.

Look for ways that you can implement games into your daily activities. Instead of sitting around watching TV after dinner, play a game with your family to keep everyone distracted from depressive thoughts. Or, try doing word searches, sudoku, and crosswords to give you something to do with your hands. Adult coloring books are great as well.

Relaxed Detective

The following is a good exercise to center yourself and bring you to a calm state of mindfulness. Think of yourself as a detective looking for clues. Absorb the details of your surroundings. Notice color schemes of the area—the grass and the sky or the artwork and the pictures if you happen to be inside. Notice the people around you. Are they tall? Short? Notice hair colors and styles. Taking in all the details around you from the mindset of a detective can help get you centered again.

Quote Mantra

Memorize some of your favorite quotes to repeat in your head when you get stressed and need to get to a more productive, balanced state of mind. The Tao I-Ching has some good ones, for instance.

"Sixteen spokes converge on the hub of the wheel, but it is not these spokes that make the wheel useful. Rather, it is the emptiness in the middle. A potter may shape a fine vase, but it is not the vase which is important but the nothing inside which you will fill."

Quotes such as this one can help you to focus and stay centered.

The Politician Pause

Another role-play includes imagining yourself as a politician. Take your stress and give it a positive spin in your mind as if you are reporting to your constituents instead of beating yourself with it. A little practice can make this technique very useful to you—you can learn to express problems to yourself in a general abstract that helps you focus on the positive.

Fake Yawn

Have you ever had someone yawn near you and then you find yourself yawning as well? It has happened to us all, and it can be surprisingly useful for a quick and solid dose of Mindfulness. Make a slow, fake yawn and you can induce this behavior in yourself. This gives you an instant splash of a meditative, relaxed state, and that small dose is sometimes all you need to find your focus.

Body Scan

The technique is often assisted, but it can be done alone as well. You should lie on your back, palms held at your sides. The scan begins by focusing on your breathing. Note the rhythm of your breath before focusing on the feeling in your feet, then your legs, and up along your body.

Take note of how it feels to move your toes and the feel of the exercise mat underneath you. Note any aches or pains as you slowly scan your body. Finally, when you've scanned your body in this manner and arrived at your head, finish by taking note of how your scalp feels against the pillow. Open your eyes and you will find yourself mindful and refreshed.

Listening Mindfully

This exercise is normally done in a group, but with couples who are very close and open with each other (or wish to be), it can be an immensely useful tool for obtaining a meditative state of understanding and mindfulness both with the self and with the other. It begins with sitting close together. Each person speaks, uninterrupted, about one thing that they are stressed about as well as something that they are looking forward to enjoying. When the first finishes, the other speaks about their own single stress and the thing that they are looking forward to enjoying.

The person speaking at the time should focus on their feelings about speaking and what they are saying—how their mind races or how their body feels. They should also focus on the posture of the other during their talk. The listener should focus on how they feel listening and on the speaker's body language. Thus, personal body language can be learned, which is useful enough for the whole exercise, but there is much more to be obtained from this practice.

At the close of the practice, each person describes what it was like for them both to speak and to listen. Some points to consider: How did I feel while talking? While listening? Did my mind wander at all? Did I feel judged or pass judgment?

For couples, a good closing might be for each to repeat what the other person said using their own words. No judgment should be made, but some positive affirmation can be given. Examples of closing remarks are: "Yes, that is close to/exactly what I was wanting to communicate" or "I don't feel that was everything, but we'll keep working at this so that we may both be heard."

Don't expect results overnight, but with this technique, closeness and mindfulness can be improved in the couple structure. Like anything worthwhile, a little work is involved, but you will love the results.

Life Savers

Take the first roll of candy apart and assign a particular moment of success or happiness to a color in the candy stack. Taste each flavor as you assign it as this is important to achieve the desired effect.

When you are feeling disjointed, tasked, or stressed, take a Life Saver out of your pocket, note the color, and then taste it. Think of the happy moment you've associated with it. Don't overthink it, just taste the flavor and think of your happy place, time, or moment. Savor it, enjoy the candy, and do not let yourself think of the problem until the Life Saver is finished.

Giving yourself a break to think of something positive can help you get your mind back to the logical and positive approach to life. Creating a mental reminder in the candy can help you draw upon that memory in an instant through a physical medium. Plus, the candy is portable.

Raisin

Less associated to specific feelings, the "raisin" is another popular Mindfulness technique associated with taste that can help you bring your mind to the surface over emotional turmoil or the perils of anxiety. This technique involves taking a raisin and pretending that it is the first time you have ever had one. Note how it feels in your hand and its texture when squeezed between your fingers. How does it smell? Lick it. How does it taste before you bite into it? After? The simple act of slowing down and contemplating all of the stages of enjoying this fruit can have a calming effect on the thoughts, distracting you for a moment and bringing a proper state of mindfulness to your thoughts.

Five Senses

"Five Senses" is another great technique that requires nothing but your body. For this one, don't get up and grab things, but instead, just identify them in your mind. This method takes you through all five of your senses, the ability to hear, see, touch, smell, and taste. You will also be counting down from five, so there will be less of a chance to be interrupted by more intrusive thoughts.

Start by identifying five things that you can see. These are any five things, and you just have to pick them out with your brain and your eyes. Maybe it is the couch in front of you, or the table that is holding all your stuff.

Next, find four things that you can touch. Maybe it is your own leg, or perhaps the fuzzy blanket wrapped around you. After that, pick out three things that you can hear. Perhaps the wind is knocking against the windows, or maybe there's a dog barking outside.

Now find two things that you can smell. You might not be able to smell anything easily, like a candle or perfume, but maybe the couch you are sitting on has a smell, or perhaps you live above a coffee shop.

Finally, pick out one thing that you can taste. You shouldn't actually taste this item, but there is something in the room you are in that has a flavor, so what is it? What would you be able to identify that item by? Repeat this process as often as you need to keep you grounded in the present moment.

Stage Breath

This technique is simple to do, and its appeal is that it is quick, portable, and effective. When distressed and needing some quick relief, simply breathe in, counting to three. Hold the breath and count to three. Then exhale, stopping when you reach a count of three. You can alternate the counts for various results, but three will get you started. Try different counts for the steps to see which results are best for you. Some inhale for three, hold for three, and exhale for four. Some do the opposite. Find what works for you. This technique also works in pain management, and practice can make it become automatic when your body and mind find it useful on a subconscious level.

Chapter 7 Dealing With Guilt

Take Responsibility But Don't Blame Yourself

There is a huge difference between taking responsibility and blaming yourself. The difference here is that blaming yourself is creating more problems and burdens for yourself. Your mind becomes heavy and troubled when you start playing the blame game. You will end up becoming the victim and the guilty. That's too much pressure for your health and it may end up breaking you down the more. Blaming yourself is raining guilt on yourself and giving your mind more works to do. This will not help you under your current circumstance. Becoming the guilty victim is not going to get you anywhere with guilt, so, the best thing you can do is to be one at most. However, try not to be the guilty. You can embrace yourself as the victim but not as the guilty. Being the guilty might make you conclude that you are facing your karma and there's nothing you or anybody can do about it. However, that's not true; that's just your mind playing its role in the side you have decided to take.

On the other hand, taking the role of the victim and also taking responsibility for your health and whatever that happened will give you the strength to find a way out. Deciding to take responsibility will lead you into making plans that will guide your healing process. Depression and anxiety disorders are also fueled by guilt, but when you take responsibility without blaming yourself, you give your mind strength and courage to face whatever it is that is confronting you. Deliberately and actively pursue a solution to whatever it is that happened and you will feel better in the end.

Don't worry about things you cannot control

Worrying never get anything solved, it only compounds it and makes you hurt the more. You need to understand when things are beyond your control and stop worrying about them as much as you need to take responsibility for the things that happen around you, there are some that are not within your ability, don't worry over them. Worrying is only going to get you more pains and that is one thing you don't need in your life. Worrying can also cause you to make even more mistakes because you become incapable of making rational decisions and this may end up hurting you them more. You cannot take care of everything just as you cannot fix everything, therefore, you need to stop beating yourself up over things that you know you cannot do anything about. Worrying about such things is going to make you feel like it's your fault even when you have no idea what went wrong. Having a sense of responsibility to try to fix things is good, but worrying over things that are beyond you is never the best way to handle it.

When things go wrong, it's okay to feel concerned and want to help. Before you jump into worrying yourself out, identify the problem, if there's one, take note of it. The next thing is to ascertain the nature of the problem. Once you have ascertained the problem, then, go on to finding out if there's anything you can do it help. If there is nothing you can do, then, go ahead and do it. But if you find that there is nothing you can do, please try not to break your head over it. It is obvious that you can't really do anything to help out. Give the moral support that you can give and try not to worry.

Forgive yourself

Something wrong happened or someone hurts you, it is not the time to burry yourself in tears and punish yourself with guilt. It is possible that you made the mistake and it's entirely your fault, that's fine. Everyone at one point or the other has actually made mistakes that have costs a thing or two; you're not alone in that. Making mistakes is one of the things that make you human and it is also one of the things that will help you grow. If you haven't made any mistake in life, then, it means you have actually not started living. It is impossible to go through life without making one bad decision or the other. The way to deal with such things like this is to forgive yourself and move on. If you messed up and as such didn't do well, learn to forgive yourself and shake off the blames that are creeping into your head. Don't lock yourself up in the prison of your subconscious and expect anything good to happen. Learning to forgive yourself is going to bring you a lot more peace of mind and keep further health challenges from resulting or triggering episodes.

When other people are at fault or wrong you, you still need to learn to forgive them. Unforgiveness is going to keep you bitter and sad. If someone hurts you and you refuse to forgive the person, you will end up giving them the power to hurt you over and over again each time you see them or remembers what happened. Not forgiving people for the things they did to you is one easy way to stay angry. You are surrounding yourself with negative energies that will make you feel bad eventually and serve as a perfect trigger for another depressive or anxiety episodes. Rather than holding on to people and locking yourself in the prison of your subconscious, just forgive them and move on with your life.

You will feel some warm when you forgive. When you have feelings of guilt that you cannot explain where they are coming from, you may have to take a little tour through your mind. All you have to do is take a retrospect and introspect of your life from as far back as you can remember. This tour is like taking a walk through time; you can call your own time travel. The essence of this is to look places where you did something wrong and have not made any corrections of your mistakes. Our pasts have a way of catching up on us in the near future. You have to make peace with yourself and help yourself get better so you can move on. There is need for you to reconcile with your past because your past has a way of putting limits on your present and denying you of a good future. Make your findings and make peace. One way to reconcile is to forgive yourself for the wrong you did at the time and find out if there is any consequence that is lingering. If there is any, then, you need to find a way to stop it otherwise you'll have still hunting you.

Generally, unforgiveness will cloak the mind and deny the heart of love thereby leaving your heart cold and cruel. Forgiveness gives your heart so much warmth and let you find peace within.

You Need to Learn to Let Go

The human mind is a library with enough shelves for as many experiences that you let in. when bad things happen to you, when people hurt you, it has a way of registering in your mind and you can use that against them. Sadly, they are not the only ones that get the impact of your mind holding back to those memories; you too get hurt. When you have a health condition such as depression and anxiety disorder, the last thing you want weighing on your mind are memories of people who hurt you at one time or the other. The memories alone can hunt you and hurt you more than the actual incident did. This is why you need to learn to let go. The moment you have forgiven, the next thing is to let go. If memories like that stay in your head, there are high chances that you will struggle with guilt. You may end up feeling guilty for letting them hurt or feeling guilty for every other pains you've been through. Don't guilt trip yourself by holding on to things that hurt you. The individuals that hurt you might be living their best lives and enjoying it, why you deny yourself opportunities because of what might have been your fault.

I'm not going to sit down here and conclude that it is easy to let go, letting go might be the hardest thing you can ever have to do, but it will be worth it in the end. The process of letting go begins with deciding to let go. The moment you decide to let go and actually means it, your mind will start working on it and as you consciously ignores it, you will find yourself letting go. This will help you get out of whatever hold it had on you. You can't let go unless you first decide to let go. The power of choice remains the key in this process.

Manage Hostility and Criticism

We live in a world where people would naturally criticize what they don't understand and what they don't appreciate. If you are waiting for a pat on your back all the time, then, get ready to be disappointed for the rest of your life. You can always get out of any condition you find yourself if you put your mind to it. Man will always be man and criticism and hostility is already part of man. You don't have to let them put you down. The following steps can help you manage criticism and hostility.

For Valid and Constructive Criticism

Not ever criticism is bad but as a person with depression and anxiety disorder, you may see every criticism as a direct attack on your health. When criticisms are valid and are constructively given, there is need for you to listen as you might find useful in the long run. All you have to do is focus on what the person is saying while you calm yourself. At this point you may be tempted to react to the criticism, but if you calm yourself down and pay attention to what the person is saying rather than whom the person is, then, you might just be able get past it. If you let yourself become distracted by the fact that the person is criticizing you, the chances are that you will miss out the validity in the critique and may snap at the person or even at yourself and this will end up hurting you the more.

For Invalid and Destructive Criticism

When you are being criticized and you know that the person's criticism is invalid and aimed at attacking you person, you don't have to snap. The right thing to do at this point is to focus on calming yourself than paying attention to what the other person is saying. The more you pay attention to the person's destructive comments the more you feel bad and hurt. Remember that it is not about the person, but about you. Because of this you cannot afford to let the person's negative comments mess with your head. Stay calm and ignore the comments.

When Criticism is Unfair

There are times when criticism is unfair and you are right, it is not a time to feel bad and worried. Clarify and explain yourself but try not spend time apologizing. When you stand your ground and explain yourself so that people see things your way, it gives you a positive feeling. You feel a lot better than when you just stand and apologize even when you know that you are right and they are just being unfair. Some criticism may make you feel like you don't know what you are doing, you have to learn to stand your ground instead of give in to the want to make you feel.

When Criticism Is Aim At Attacking You

You know when someone is just being a bully or being hostile to you. When you face such persons, the best thing to do is to ignore whatever it is they are saying and try not to react at all. Walk away from them and let them call you a coward if they want to. You are only protecting yourself against what may likely cause you more pains.

When People use nonverbal cues to criticize you or try to make you feel bad, instead of actually feeling bad ask for clarifications. They may be embarrassed trying to explain themselves most of them don't have the courage to actually face you or even speak up, they would rather hid behind gestures.

Always try to keep moving in the face of any hostile condition. Stay in control of how you respond to people's actions and try not to let them take advantage of your health condition. The truth is some of them are in worse conditions than you and may be hiding it under their shameful acts.

Build Self-esteem

Believe in Yourself

A belief system is more than just some ideas accepted by the mind; it is a force that patterns a person's thoughts, actions and reactions and ultimately a person's way of life. Imagine if you have a belief system that is centered on smashing goals; I'm sure you'll be almost unstoppable. The best way to build self-esteem is to belief in yourself. Self-esteem is an indispensable tool that you must have if you want to deal with such mental health conditions as depression and anxiety disorders. These mental health conditions have a way of making you feel lesser than people around you. They would sometimes make you feel like you are not worth anything and drag you self-esteem so low that you might want to even end your own life. But by believing in yourself, you can boldly look in the face of any threat or challenge and walk out of it with a lot better result than you can imagine. You need to understand that you have the ability to reach beyond the limitations of your health condition. The first thing you have to do is belief in yourself and the things you are capable of. Let go of a lot of things that have made you think you can't do much, embrace a new reality, a new identity and you will find yourself forging ahead better.

Choose to be Bold

Whatever happens to you, life will always leave you with the power of choice to decide what will eventually become of you.

You can decide to cower in the identities that your health condition has created for you or you can decide to embrace a new identity. In the face of low self-esteem, the best thing you can do is to make the choice to remain bold against all odds. There will never be a time when you will find everything working for you; there are times when your flames will be burn low and you find yourself falling down a cliff. The stigma attached to your health condition might break you into a thousand pieces, but you need to understand at such points that you are just going through a face and you alone have the power to determine its outcome. Choose to stand up bold and embrace your new identity. When you are booed, take it as the crowd waiting for you to rise, because when you do, the same people that booed you will give you a loud ovation. When you match boldness with self-believe, you are on your way to rising beyond your limitation and you will definitely feel better with each successful stride.

Pay More Attention to Your Journey than What People are Saying

Whether you succeed or fail, people will always have some negative comments to make. You cannot afford to ears drop or pay attention to the words of every Tom, Dick and Harry. Even those who care about you and actually mean well for sometimes may even say negative things to you and about you. This is to tell you that there is no room for failure. You are on a journey and may not even see it that way and that's why you keep listening to the side talks about you. These side talks are the distractions that keep you from focusing on your journey. If you keep listening to what people have to say about you because you have are suffering depression or anxiety disorder, you will end up worse. In order to keep your self-esteem high, you must listen more to yourself, your therapist and your process. These are some of the three major things that can help you keep moving ahead. Your journey is the most important and you have to trust every process on the way. To build your self-esteem, your own voice should matter more to you than the voice of those around you. You have to learn to depend less on people and more on yourself. This is that time in your life when you are allowed to be overly independent as long as it keeps you from depending on people for everything and being distracted by negative comments. If you become dependent on people, you may never be able to deal with a lot of things on your own because you will always fear you cannot do them on your own.

Make the process count and let yourself heal through your personal efforts. The more positive results you achieve on your own, the more you will be building your self-esteem and the better you will become.

Chapter 8 Mindsets

The self-perceptions and beliefs you have about yourself are termed mindsets. These perceptions or beliefs that you hold about yourself will determine your mental attitude, the outlook you have about life in general, the way you approach the situations you're faced with and determine the behavior you exhibit in response to what you're going through. When you believe you can achieve something and you accomplish it, you have the right mindset to make it happen. If you believe you can't do something, then you won't because your mindset held you back.

The Growth Mindset

Individuals with a Growth Mindset believe that their basic abilities can be strengthened and developed through hard work and dedication. This notion forms the core of their belief system. To these individuals, talent and brains are only the beginning.

Out of the two, the Growth Mindset is the one you want to work on developing. This mindset is the one that lets you embrace the failures and setbacks you experience, seeing them as lessons to be learned from. This is the mindset that allows you to critically analyze, change, and adapt your behavior to suit the situation. This is the mindset that will strongly influence the kind of success you achieve throughout your life. Individuals with the

Growth Mindset stand firm on the notion that effort matters most, and they are willing to learn, adapt, grow, and do whatever it takes to get what they want. They are resilient and bold, never backing down in the face of a challenge. That's the kind of mindset you need to strive for now as you work to overcome your anxiety.

The Fixed Mindset

On the other hand, individuals with a Fixed Mindset believe that talent and intelligence are traits you get from birth (fixed). They let these beliefs define their success or failure since they spend more time documenting what their talents are instead of doing something about them. They don't work at developing the talents they have since they believe these qualities are "fixed" from birth. You either have them or you don't.

These individuals will often use phrases like dumb or brilliant when they talk about themselves. Since they believe that there is no way to change these qualities, they tend to shy away from challenges they think they are destined to fail. When they're faced with an obstacle, it's not uncommon for them to say, "I can't do this!" or "I'm going to fail". They make excuses and try to justify their reasons for rejecting the challenge.

Focusing on the Moment

For most people, half the time we spend awake, we spend thinking or worrying about something. We're not focused on the present, and we're not actively thinking about what we do.

We either go through the motions automatically, or we rush through without paying attention. We're simply not paying attention enough. As it turns out, approximately 50% of the time, these participants found that their minds were not focused on their current task. Moreover, the participants realized that wandering minds led to greater levels of unhappiness since they were not focused on the task at hand.

Why are we less than happy when our mind is wandering? Probably because a lot of the time there's a lot of "noise" going on. Memories, rehashing past events, worries about the future, formulating scenarios that have not even happened (or might not ever happen) yet. The problem is, getting swept up in our thoughts is so easy to do. Like a tide that carries you out to sea, it is almost impossible to resist the pull. The deeper your thoughts drag you into their fold, the harder it is to escape. We know this kind of thought pattern is not good for us, and it's not doing our mental health any favors either. Yet, in many ways, it's addictive. If it wasn't, we wouldn't spend so much time worrying or feeling anxious.

Focusing on the moment. That's what you need to do to take back control. It's a simple concept, yet one that is highly effective. By being focused on the present, you can do a lot to change your thoughts and with it, the emotions you feel. Pull your mind back each time it wanders and train yourself to focus on the present by:

Meditating - You'll notice that this method is encouraged a lot when you're trying to overcome your anxiety. But this is by far one of the best methods out there that gives your mind the training it needs to learn how to focus on the present. Meditation is not always about sitting in silence and trying not to think about anything as you will yourself to relax. On the contrary, meditation is linked to a myriad of psychological and neurological benefits. By being mindful and deliberately slowing down our thoughts, we're quieting the areas in the brain that is responsible for all that unnecessary noise and chatter. Trying to sit in silence and not let your scattered thoughts take center stage is going to be hard at first, but it gets easier with practice. All you need to do is find something to focus on, and in meditation, that focus can be your breath or a mantra that you repeat. Each time your mind starts to wander (and it will), don't get stressed about it. Stay calm, and simply return to focusing on your breath or mantra. That's what practice is all about.

Talking - Anytime you feel you need a shoulder to cry on, talk to someone. Being stuck in your negative thoughts is not always easy to overcome alone, and part of developing a Growth Mindset is learning to recognize when you need help. Talking about your problems can be therapeutic. It gives you some release, a way to channel the emotions that you've been keeping locked away inside. If you've ever tried this method before, do you notice how much better it feels to get something off your chest? Not to mention how having someone to talk to can put things in a different perspective and shed a different light on a situation. The very act of talking about it can turn your incoherent thoughts around so you, in turn, can understand them better. Not only is this a tool in helping you overcome the mindset that has been holding you back all this time but seeing your thoughts in a different way helps you develop a new relationship with them too. Perhaps instead of seeing them as the enemy, these thoughts can now be viewed as the very thing needed to encourage you to make a change for the better.

Take Away the Resistance - If you've been resistant to change all this time out of fear, it's time to remove that resistance so you can move forward. Resistance will only hold you back from living in the moment. You can't focus on the present if you refuse to accept it. Even if it is a situation you don't like or don't want to be in, don't resist it. That only makes it harder to be mindful and be present. You may not like where you are right now but being focused on the moment is the only way you're going to be able to change your reality.

Don't Multitask - It's ineffective. You may think you're productive, but you're not. Why? Because multitasking means your attention and focus is pulled in several directions all at once. Concentration means you're only focusing on one thing at a time. The demanding and hectic pace of today's lifestyle has led to the false belief that you're increasing your productivity when you multitask. Nothing could be further from the truth. Our minds were only made to focus on one thing, one stimulus at a time.

Discipline - Excuses are for someone who lacks discipline, and if you're serious about overcoming your anxiety once and for all, it's time to leave the excuses at the door where they belong. Holding on to your excuses only gives you a reason to continue to worry, fret, and indulge in the negative behavior patterns that are not helping you in any way. Excuses will be the reason you struggle to develop a Growth Mindset if you let it. Discipline means staying focused on what you need to do and pushing aside everything else that threatens to distract you.

Detaching from the Results of Your Goal - Goals can be confusing. Since goals are a future event and something that has not happened yet, how do you focus on the present if you need to think about your goal? By thinking of your goal as a direction. A compass that points which way you should be going. You know the outcome you want to achieve. What you need to do now is focus on what can be done in the present to get you to that final outcome. Let's say, for example, that your goal is to eventually buy a home. By becoming fixated on the result (the home), you're falling into the trap of only thinking about that outcome without doing anything about it. Have a goal but detach yourself from the result. Let the house be the final result, but that's it. Focus on where you are in life right now and what actions need to be taken so you can turn that vision into reality one day.

Affirmations and Visualization

Affirmations and visualization are exercises in changing your mindset. If you're not happy with the mindset you have now, then clearly something needs to change. Besides working on developing the Growth Mindset, other approaches that are going to prove useful to you in this process are affirmations and visualization.

How Affirmations Work

Affirmations are essentially a set of positive, empowering statements. You repeat these statements to yourself often enough until they eventually influence your subconscious mind. The idea is to keep repeating these affirmations until you adopt this new set of beliefs. If you want to be happier, then your affirmation statement might sound like this: I am positive, and I am happy every day. French psychologist Émile Coué had a wonderful positive affirmation that is ideal for anyone wanting to achieve overall life improvements in general. His affirmation was this: "Every day in every way, I am getting better and better." Beautiful, simplistic, and effective. Exactly the kind of affirmation you need to change the way you think.

For affirmations to be effective, you need to believe in them. Really believe in them and not spout them off because it's something you have to do. If you're repeating a statement that deep down you don't believe in, you're not going to convince your mind to change. Your conscious mind is powerful, and it can easily overrule any affirmation that you try to feed it if you don't believe in it. Try to tell yourself "I am rich" but the little voice in your head says, "No, you're not" is not going to result in any positive change in your life or your mindset. You could repeat the same affirmation a thousand times a day, and it's still not going to do you any good.

The subconscious mind is a mix of repetition and emotion, but the thing is, you need to feed your mind with statements it can accept. That's how you get it to change.

How Visualization Works

While affirmations are all about statements you either repeat in your mind or say out loud, visualizations work a little differently. This time, you're going to be creating images in your mind, rather than focus on the statements. This can be carried out in two ways. The first is to envision with clarity the images that you want, like the perfect life, or excelling in your career. In your mind's eye, picture all those things already happening to you as if they were already your reality. The second method is to create vision boards if having something physical to see in front of you works better. Both methods are effective. It's just a matter of which one works best for you. Some people may find vision boards more effective because of the actual imagery they can see in front of them. That makes it more real in their minds.

Visualization is an exercise that helps you focus your mind on the positive outcomes that you want to achieve. Seeing these happy images in your mind keeps you focused and motivated to do something about it, so they don't remain just visions in your mind. The idea behind visualization is that your mind is powerful enough to conjure up any image that you want. Anything is possible if you can think about it and picture it clearly. Every detail, down the finest, matters because it's the secret to making visualization work. Each one of us has the capacity to visualize. It's not a skill that is only limited to a certain few. As a child, you used to engage in pretend to play all the time. It was a major part of your childhood. Along the way, as we matured and became adults, we forgot about this and focused only on what we can see in front of us. If we can physically see it, then it's real, and that was it. Life got in the way, and visualization slowly fell by the wayside as "adult responsibilities" took precedence.

Now, the good news here is that while these imaginative skills may have become dormant along the way, we never lost the innate ability. It's still there inside of us. We only need to tap into it again and wake it up from its dormant slumber. When you're visualizing, you're telling the universe what you want. You're putting positive energy out there and using your mind to manifest the many ways you can make that vision come true. Where there's a will, there's always a way, and there is always a way to achieve something if you want it bad enough. The danger with visualization is that if you're not careful, it can take on a negative life of its own. Instead of visualizing the positive outcomes, when your emotions take over, your thoughts can be steered towards the negative. Oh boy, it is easy to be swayed over to the negative! Our minds are biased towards the negative, and it's going to take considerable effort to keep your thoughts on a positive momentum. Difficult, yes. But it can be done.

How to Successfully Visualize and Affirm

You don't need to repeat your affirmations or visualize 50 times a day for it to work. You only need to choose a few affirmations that you believe in best and repeat them for several minutes a day. The time of day you choose to do this doesn't matter either. You can do it in the morning, at night before you go to bed, or any time of the day you have a couple of minutes to spare. As long as they are statements you can believe in, that's good enough.

Other tips for making visualization and affirmations work for you are:

To pour emotion into your affirming statements. With each statement, pour your heart and soul into it. Say it with feeling and say it with conviction. Say it with love and say it with passion.

Recite your affirming statements with confidence. Push away any doubt that tries to inch their way in and squash them down by repeating your statements with even more determination.

Use present tenses with your affirmations. Not past tense, not future tense, but present tense. It's another way of teaching yourself to focus on the moment. Past tenses imply that nothing can be done about it since it's in the past. Future tense means you're focused on the outcome, which, as we've learned, you need to detach from. Have a goal without becoming fixated on the outcome. To do that, use present tenses to describe your affirmations.

Desire the images that you visualize. Want them to happen so badly that you put every ounce of energy you have left in that image you are conjuring in your mind.

Don't limit your visualization by thinking that it is impossible. It only seems far-fetched because you don't have the tools you need yet to make it happen. You will get there eventually, but for now, you need to visualize the outcome you want so you can think about what must be done.

When affirmations and visualization are done correctly, they can do a lot to remove the anxieties, worries, doubts, and fear that linger in your mind. In its place, they bestow the strength and confidence you need to turn your mindset around. When done correctly, they could be exactly what you need to find the motivation and energy to overcome your anxiety for good.

Changing Your Mindset

Your mind will determine your success. What you think you will become. Believe you're going nowhere in life, and that's exactly what will happen. Believe that you're destined for success, and success will find its way to you. We often underestimate how powerful the inner monologue of the mind can be. But think about this for a moment. If you can envision all the catastrophic outcomes with clarity - and on the rare occasion it does happen, you think, "See! I knew this would happen!" - then you can do the opposite too. The Growth Mindset the driving force that people rarely ever talk about. It can drive you to success, or it can drive you to failure. The difference is going to boil down to which mindset you allow yourself to hold onto.

Chapter 9 The Power of Perception

While Stoicism is famous for the approach it takes with regards to emotions, or lack thereof, the truth is that the real power of Stoicism comes in its logical and pragmatic approach to dealing with reality.

The Stoics believed in dealing with the world as it actually exists. This might seem to be a simple-minded statement but once you come to understand what this means you'll understand the profound implications.

If you want to find a solution, you must first size up the problem with clear and objective eyes. Doing anything less will only set you up for failure.

The Distance Between the World and Our Perception

The Stoics believed that there were three disciplines that were required to live a Stoic lifestyle. The first was perception, the second action, and the third will. This order is not an accident, there is a reason that perception is considered to be the primary discipline of Stoicism.

Perception is all about seeing the world as it actually is. It is about looking at reality as objectively as possible, taking value judgements out of the picture.

If you ask most people about how accurately they perceive the world they will tell you that they see things perfectly clear. After all, if they have two healthy eyes how else would they see things? But perception isn't just about your physical sight, it's about the way your mind processes the information you take in when you gaze out at the world.

The mind processes visual information in two steps. The first is when the light bouncing off of the object enters the eye and you perceive the reality in front of you visually. The second step is when your brain takes the image and applies a label to it. This second step is where the trouble comes in.

The problem isn't looking at a duck and calling it a duck. The trouble is that we look at tasks in front of us and we quickly jump to conclusions over whether they are possible or not. We look at people just long enough to take in their appearance and then decide whether or not we can trust them. We look at ourselves and judge what we are capable of without any solid reasoning backing up our conclusions.

Humans are driven to make judgements and our judgments are often far from the mark. This is what the Stoics understood, and it's why they put such an emphasis on correcting our perception so that we see the world as it actually is before we try and act within it.

First Day on The Job

To help understand the destructive nature of inaccurate perception I will walk you through a scenario. Imagine that you are showing up to your first day at a new job and you are meeting with your coworkers. In this scenario you are a rather judgmental person who is prone to quickly jumping to conclusions about everyone you meet.

You walk into the office and the first person you meet is your new boss. He shakes your hand, but his grip is a little limp. You immediately label him as weak before moving onto the next person. The first coworker you meet has a smile on their face but a stain on their shirt. The word "slob" comes to mind before you leave that person to meet another. The final person you meet greets you kindly but has a monotone voice, so you can't help but think of them as boring.

Now, think about how those instantly generated labels might impact your future working relationships with those individuals. Conclusions you jumped to in this scenario based on next to no information could color your interactions with your coworkers for years to come.

Hopefully you are now beginning to see how easily our perception can become clouded by an over-eagerness to judge the world around us. The untrained mind jumps to conclusions almost instantly, but the judgements it doles out can linger for days, weeks, or even years.

Slow to Judge and Slow to Trust

While some people may already be on board with a more objective approach to reality, I know that there will be others who are reluctant. You might have read through the "First Day on the Job" segment and felt that the character in the scenario was right to make those judgements. Often people will defend these sorts of judgements on practical grounds. There are a lot of people out there, some of them have bad intentions, and if you wait for such individuals to reveal their bad intentions before taking precautions then you will be left at their will.

This is a fair point, but it misses the point of delaying judgement. Many people assume that if you won't label someone as dishonest then you are declaring that they are honest. But this simply isn't the case. You can withhold both positive and negative judgments at the same time. If you don't know someone well, you can withhold both trust and distrust until you've gotten a chance to get a better idea of who they are as a person.

Remember that Stoicism is about engaging with the world in a rational and logical way. If you know you are entering an area where crime is common you don't have to pretend like this information is unavailable to you. If reason says that safety precautions should be taken, then by all means, take safety precautions.

Still, consider where you are getting your information from. Are you judging the risk level based on objective information or snap judgements based off of personal biases? People tend to overrate their own objectivity.

The fact is that it takes time and energy to cultivate the ability to see the world as it actually is. For most people, it's not like a switch that can be flipped on or off, even if you can withhold judgement for a while you might find yourself sliding back into old habits before too long. But there's no reason to despair. Stoicism isn't about quick and easy solutions; it's about taking the time to bring about true and lasting change.

A Shift in Perception

Once you take the time to pay attention to the way that you perceive the world and shape it with your thoughts, you will come to realize just how much power you have. The only unfortunate thing is that you may only realize this once you recognize that you have been holding yourself back from your full potential with unwarranted negative thinking.

The good news is that it's never too late to make a change. As long as you are still drawing breath, you can take command of your thoughts and use them to reshape your world.

Turning the World Upside Down

There is a trick in the art world for anyone who wants to draw a complex image but feels overwhelmed when they look at it. The trick is taking the image and flipping it upside down. Suddenly the person no longer feels like they are drawing an entire head, instead they see it as drawing a field of individual shapes. When you wipe words like "difficult" or "impossible" out of the picture and focus on the individual steps, you might be amazed at what you can achieve.

The same can be said for examining your life. The average person looks at the events that lay ahead of them and focuses in on anything that seems like it will be a challenge or an obstacle. Once we label them as problems they tend to grow in our minds, becoming outsized threats that loom over us and cause unwarranted stress.

But what if you could turn the image upside down? What if you could look out at what you would normally call obstacles and call them opportunities instead?

Transforming a Cage into a Tool

The sad fact is that most people are trapped by their own perception. Years of bias and mental programming has made it difficult for them to see the world as it is. Even worse, when they look at the world, they see so many insurmountable obstacles that they feel hopelessly restrained.

They are like a person who puts on a virtual reality headset and ends up trapped in an open field. Even though no physical walls surround them they still feel restrained because of the walls they see in their head.

Learning to see the world objectively is like taking off the headset. It shows you the full range of movement available to you. But you don't have to stop there. Taking control of your perception is like reprogramming that virtual reality headset to help you find where you're going. This is the full power of mastering your perception, you can reshape the way you see the world in a way that propels you forward rather than holding you back.

Eliminating Worry

Mastering perception is an especially helpful tool for anyone who struggles with worry. After all, what causes worry? Most people experience this feeling after they identify potential problems in their life and allow these potential issues to haunt their mind. As long as the issue goes unaddressed it remains a worry, floating through your conscious and wreaking havoc.

The problem with worries is that there is no limit to how many you can have. You might think you could cure them by solving your problems, but once the human mind has been trained to look for potential problems it will always find more. This is why it helps to be able to retrain your brain. Once you do there is almost no limit to what you might achieve.

Separating Acceptance from Agreement

Before we move on from perception, we need to discuss a related issue, acceptance. Stoicism is built around accepting the world as it is. This is tied in with perception. The idea is that in order to perceive the world as it really is you have to be prepared to accept it as it truly is. Those who feel like the world must be a certain way will find ways to distort their perception in order to try and square their beliefs with the external world. This is something that Stoicism can't accept.

Stoicism says that any philosophy that doesn't rest on a foundation of actual reality is like a house built on sand. No matter how sturdy it may look, the lack of a solid foundation will doom it in the end.

This is why true Stoics must accept the world as it is. Doing anything else would endanger your perception and threaten everything else that comes down the line. However, it's worth noting that acceptance does not mean agreement.

The Case for Stoic Action

It's easy to fall into the trap of thinking that Stoicism is a defeatist philosophy. The idea of a Stoic who accepts fate can conjure up an image of surrendering to the powers that be, allowing other people to take control and heading off into the mountains to meditate while the world burns. But this couldn't be further from the truth.

One of the reasons it's important to study Marcus Aurelius is because he wasn't just a great thinker, he was a man of action. He embodied the Stoic practice of acceptance while acting as the emperor of the ancient world's preeminent superpower. He didn't just stand by and accept it when the Gauls attacked Rome, he led his forces out and battled.

This leaves us with a question, was Marcus a hypocrite when he shaped the future for him and his people? Are Stoics being hypocrites when they rail against some elements of human nature while promoting others? The answer is a resounding "no!"

Understanding the Reason Behind the Mantra

The Stoics continually point out the things that individuals cannot change in order to emphasize the things that they can. The "fate" that is to be accepted isn't everything in reality, it's everything beyond our own sphere of influence.

This sphere's core is our own behavior, the one thing in life that we have anywhere near total control. Beyond that, we have the people and things around us that we can interact with. This is an area where we have some influence, but we don't ultimately have control in the same way that have control over our own thoughts and actions. Beyond this second layer is the rest of the universe, which is completely within the hands of fate.

Take a moment to think about this. There are over 6 billion people on this planet. How many do you know or interact with on a regular basis? Even if you regularly interact with thousands of people, that's still less than one percent of one percent of the world's population. In the grand scheme of things, most human activity is beyond our ability to control or even influence in any real way. But does that mean that it isn't worth trying?

Stoicism isn't just about self-help. It's a philosophy oriented around virtue, and virtue has always been understood to be a community project. The person who lives alone on a desert island rarely gets a chance to display the sort of virtues that someone in a community can practice every day.

So, while Stoicism asks that you accept the world as it exists at this point in time, it doesn't mean that the world must always remain the way it is. On the contrary, Stoics understand that the only real constant is change. The world is in flux and you as an individual are compelled to act in a virtuous manner, for the sake of yourself, your community, and your world.

Stoics have brought about real change throughout history and there's no reason for this trend to stop with you. The beauty of Stoicism is that once you stop to gain control of your own mind you can achieve levels of efficacy that you might never have dreamed about before. Thoughtless flailing is replaced with carefully considered action. Emotionalism is traded in for a logical commitment to your cause.

And finally, the obstacles that once held you back can be transformed. Events that seemed like problems become opportunities, helping you chart a course into the future that you never would have thought possible without Stoic thinking.

Careful thought can allow you to stop worrying about circumstances that are beyond your control and focus in on those that are within your ability to command. You can stop wasting time, energy, and resources on pointless worry and start becoming a more effective and fulfilled human being. This sort of transformation isn't quick or easy, but it can improve your life immeasurably if you're willing to commit to it.

So, you see, Stoics may have to accept the current reality but that doesn't mean they have to agree with it. They are free to work to bring about change, and the skills developed by practicing Stoicism actually make it easier to achieve real results in this world.

Practical Takeaway

Using your powers of perception to turn obstacles into opportunities is one of the most powerful weapons in a Stoic's arsenal. If you want to master this ability, then you should start practicing as soon as possible.

Take out your paper and writing utensil. Now, take the time and write down an obstacle or problem you have been worrying about lately.

Once you have finished writing the problem down, take another moment to reexamine the situation you are dealing with more objectively. Describe it in cold and technical terms, avoiding emotion or any other powerful language.

Now take things one step further and consider how the objective situation you are dealing with might offer some hidden opportunity.

If you have gone through these steps, then you will have taken a source of worry in your life and turned it into an opportunity to develop as a human being. This is a process you can use time and time again throughout your day. There is no telling how many opportunities you might uncover if you learn how to master your perception.

Chapter 10 Cognitive Behavioral Therapy and Dialectical Behavior Therapy

Everyone is insecure; everyone has their own stuff they deal with on a consistent basis; everyone deals with the same emotions. You need to understand that even the most beautiful people in the world are insecure, how do I know this?

I have been around a lot of people in my life and I have had the privilege of interviewing models and people that you would think have it all together. I interviewed this one lady who told me that even though she is in all of the magazine's looking flawless it's all been photo shopped to look perfect. 'I don't look like what the magazine does me up to look like. I'm a human being who has flaws like everyone and sometime I feel like I'm more insecure because I feel like I have to live up to looking like the magazine perception every day.' I even see in magazine that they have fitness models telling you to look a certain way. The best fitness model in the world Greg Plitt said to never read a fitness magazine and think the front cover is possible to reach. It's designed to make you feel insecure and motivate you to keep going up the never ending staircase.

Always remember whatever you see in magazines is usually completely fake and realize that you should be focusing on what's real instead of reaching for an impossible image. I don't care if you are 5ft tall as a male or you are a 6ft5 female, you can feel as attractive as you feel you deserve to be. Attraction is just a feeling and for most people they get so caught up believing it's all to do with the external.

I personally used to believe I wasn't attractive and I wouldn't even be able to talk to someone looking into their eye because I thought they were judging all my insecurities. I used to want to be an actor as a kid but I never had the confidence to follow through and go for it. I had an amazing teacher that was into personal development and he helped young males with their confidence. People in my class I felt were much better actors than me and half the reason was because I didn't feel comfortable in my own skin. I remember the teacher telling the whole class that we had to get up by ourselves and do a 2minute acting scene. I was traumatized because I knew everyone would judge me and I blew the situation out in my head, have you ever done that? When we were in practice my teacher come over to me and asked me how I was feeling about stepping up and really going for it. I said, 'I don't feel comfortable being an actor because right now I know everyone is watching me and judging me.' My teacher told me something that I have taken around with me my whole life. He said, 'I want you to remember this for as long as you live Jack. No one is looking at you, because they are too busy looking at judging themselves. Everyone is feeling the same way you are Jack and if you really can understand that, you have an advantage to step up.'

Realizing that no one really cares about you as much as you do can give you freedom in your life. When you go home, are you thinking about someone else's flaws or are you focusing on your own. The answer is everyone only cares about what's going on with them and they are stuck in that world of scarcity. Waiting for the day everything will get better but the day only comes if you make a decision to love yourself and let go of your flaws. Changing what your flaws mean to you. If your flaws mean your life is over and you are never going to put yourself out there because of them, then you are stuck. But if you change the meaning of what they mean to you, the whole ball changes.

I have had a good friend of mine that told me she thinks she is ugly and wishes she was someone else. What kind of thinking would it take to really think that way? To completely reject yourself and beat yourself up about things you can't control is very silly in my opinion. The way I helped her was I got her to confront herself in the mirror and tell herself three simple words, I love you. She literally couldn't do it at all and would just start crying. The total fear of acceptance was holding her back from telling herself the truth. Deep down she did love herself but by telling herself she didn't everyday she started to believe something that wasn't true. It was her opponent and by getting her to really say it, her whole face transformed. It's what she had been missing her whole life and she wasn't attracting anyone into her life because who would want to love someone who tortures themselves.

I don't know what level you are at in your life whether this is crippling you or not but you just need to accept and love yourself. Accept every flaw that you have because they make up who you are. People wait for their life to magically change but I know for a fact it'll never change unless you do something. If you are worried about your flaws today you will be worrying about them in 10 years' time. You will be older so your flaws will get worse with age and you will just keep rationalizing it'll get better.

People get stuck in indulging in negative emotions and I want you to decide today that you aren't going to hold yourself back. One big thing that people do is they compare themselves to other people which means we can never feel good about ourselves. I used to compare myself all the time to others and said to myself,' why can't I have just been a little taller because all my friends are tall. I would beat myself up over it and not even having the faith to accept myself.

If I was 6ft and my friend were 6ft3 I would be comparing myself to them and I could even make a story up in my head that says, 'if I was 3" taller I would have what I want.' We all do this and it's crazy how much this play with your head. It's the same with money. If I am making $100,000 a year and all my friends are making $300,000 a year I would be comparing myself to them and it would make me feel angry, frustrated or sad or disappointed. But if I just appreciate where I am at right now and accept myself, my life will transforms in that moment. Let me ask you how much time are you spending appreciating what's around you?

It's a shame to think that most people take their families for granted because they are so caught up in their own miserable world. I am not pointing fingers at anyone because I have had times years ago where all I would do is focus on me. In those times I couldn't even feel present when I was with people because I was obsessing about the future. My life used to be about the future and I used to tell myself, 'I am going to do all these things in the future, I am going to be happy in the future when I achieve XD.' That's the most destructive mindset that a lot of people in this world have and it ruins their relationships and personal lives. People that are struggling with depression are living like this and I was depressed a good deal of my life. It's a sick feeling that everything is happening to you and the worlds owes you something. The world doesn't owe you anything, and the only way out of the slump that we get into is work hard and enjoying the process.

The biggest change for me was enjoying the process because if you don't enjoy what you're doing everyday, how do you know you will when you get everything you've ever wanted? In life it's not about getting the goal or the external stimulus but it's about the person who you become in pursuit of you getting it. You can take all the 'things' in your life away but no one can take away the person who you become. That's why I do seminars all over teaching people to break out of their negative thinking. It doesn't do you any service but make you doubt yourself and it doesn't move you in a healthier direction.

We define the meaning to everything in our life. Whatever happens to you in your life you can either take it as a positive or a negative and most people don't define the meaning consciously so their unconscious patterns take over. Most people take what other people say to them to heart and they hold onto it unconsciously forever unless they resolve it.

I was told by my teachers in school and by a few people that I would never be anything or have the ideal person in my life. I held onto this story for nearly five years of my life and I would reject anyone that come close to me because of it. It has nothing to do with them saying something mean to you, it's about you believing what they are saying. If you know you're a strong person and someone calls you weak it won't affect you at all. But if you take what someone's says to heart, it'll destroy you emotionally.

Never let someone else's opinion of you turn into your reality because that will just keep you in victim mode and you will shut down emotionally to everyone to protect yourself. Start realizing that you're in control and stop thinking that life is happening to you and start changing the meaning of you flaws to a positive. You don't have to feel insecure. You can have an advantage of knowing that everyone is caught up with themselves to worry about you, so you can start living free today.

From all the experiences I have been through in my life, you have to be able to laugh at yourself even when you should feel afraid. If you can seriously start coming out with a sense of humour and laugh at yourself like other people are laughing, they have no power of you. Laughing cleanses the soul; it frees your mind and shoots natural endorphins through your body which makes you feel better about yourself. If you were laughing and I called you an idiot, you wouldn't be worried about it. But if you were feeling insecure you would hold onto that comment. This whole game has to do with whatever state of mind you're in because you are confident in one state and another you feel scared and frightened of the world. I know there is a part of you that just wants to let go and have fun and that's the real you. You have just been conditioned by society to feel the way you're feeling and hold back in life. I say go out there, be wild, crazy and live life on your terms; period.

Chapter 11 Being Responsible for your Mental Well-Being

So far, we have learned that anxiety and depression are conditions that are regular and painful. The feelings can range from a normal feeling down that can last for several weeks to a very severe condition that might need treatment at the hospital. CBT works with or without anti-depressant medicines and has been proven to lessen the relapse rates.

This chapter majorly focuses on the Behavioral in CBT and demonstrates to you that slowly facing up to things you are avoiding, increasingly taking part in activities you see as rewarding, and positively dealing with any sort of difficulties that you face can have a profound impact on your low mood. Along with this, we show how going over and over stuff in your mind can at times appear to be solving a means of problem-solving.

Deciding Whether You are Depressed

Recognizing common signs and symptoms of depression has numerous advantages. It can give you a stronger picture of whether you are suffering from 'the blues' or 'ups and downs' or whether you are having have symptoms of a known illness. Always create your checklist to recognize any symptoms of anxiety or depression that you face. Then, you can choose to show your checklist to your physician and discuss probable treatment options. As well, you can use it as your reference point to always get back to as you work on overcoming your depression and see how the symptoms are improving.

Assessing Your Avoidance

In this chapter, we will point out and elaborate more on the tactics that people have used to try and help themselves in feeling better that have mostly made their emotional problems to worsen. Avoiding social interaction and daily tasks are part of depression. It's very tempting to surrender to your depressed emotions and hide away from others as well as your responsibilities. Nevertheless, such avoidance often leads to living a less gratifying life, leaving you less in charge of your life, leading to financial issues mounting up, reducing your ability to solve problems, and decreasing the support you can get from others. Consider that which you might be avoiding (including chores and pleasures) and what you are doing in blocking out painful feelings and thoughts. The impact of some actions varies according to what purpose they serve. For example, enjoying a favorite TV program, might be worthwhile and be part of the mood-lifting plan, on the other hand, watching TV for endless hours to block out others and the entire world will maintain and even worsen your depression. Blocking out actions and behaviors tend to be the things you do rather than getting on with the duties that are in your best interest to handle. So, watching TV rather than answering your phone calls may be a good example of avoidance behavior and a blocking out behavior. Mostly, you will engage in blocking out behaviors as your mood will be too low so that everything seems overwhelming and pointless. Regrettably, the more one let things pile up the more their depressed increases. Blocking out behaviors also includes things like using alcohol, drugs, or food to aid in numbing your depressed emotions. These things might work in the short-term, but they frequently bring about worsened depression the following day.

Actively Attacking Your Depression

Having an activity plan is one of the most effective psychological technique one can use to actively combat depression. This tool/technique is often ignored or under-utilized by both the patients as well as their therapists because it may seem too simple, though research shows that it works effectively. An activity schedule/plan is a daily diary sheet containing times of the day visibly drawn in two-hour blocks. Becoming lively again is an important step to overcoming depression. Because depression promotes lethargy and saps motivation, the activity schedule will help you to get going with your daily tasks that you may be evading. Research indicates that this simple act of making a plan of your daily doings/activities and assigning specific times to specific tasks significantly increases the chance of carrying them out. Once one starts using an activity schedule his or her enthusiasm to do the things he or she once enjoyed and found satisfying will return gradually. You can use an activity schedule for several jobs:

- Recording weekly activity to provide a reference point to return to in future weeks for making comparisons against your progress

- Beginning to increasingly face up to things that you have been evading and becoming more stimulated

- Lessening blocking-out behaviors and substituting them with more productive or fulfilling activities.

- Organizing your day-to-day routines to give your sleeping patterns and appetite the best possible opportunity of returning to normalcy. Normally, in this case, means sleeping for roughly eight hours and taking a least 3 regular meals in a day.

- Planning your week or day to assist in getting chores done, keeping social activities, and setting aside some time for your hobbies and interests.

- Tracking that you progressively increase your activities/events realistically and steadily instead of overloading yourself with all sorts of things that you think you ought to do.

Lifting Low Self-Esteem

Rating yourself as a 'success' or a 'failure', 'good' or 'bad', 'worthy' or 'worthless' based on your circumstances or achievements is very common. Though, being a common practice does not make it a good practice. Attaching self-opinion to external factors is the main cause of self-esteem problems. Your opinion of yourself is susceptible to tumbling if your current state of affairs is not well maintained. Life is not predictable as well as prone to change, and so your view of yourself and mood might shift wildly if you steadily anchor your worth to your relationship, job, financial situation, etc. Including the term self-esteem itself is problematic as it suggests that an individual can be granted an overall rating even if the individual doing the evaluation is you! Evaluating a piece of jewelry and assessing its market value is easy. However, people are living, changing creatures as well as far more complex than non-living objects. A substitute for self-esteem is the notion of self-acceptance. CBT recommends that you to stop ranking yourself on global ratings. However, accept yourself as an essentially worthwhile person and only rank individual characteristics/aspects of yourself, your behavior, lifestyle, etc. The rules and guidelines for self-acceptance still apply to other acceptance. Working on an attitude of other acceptance can aid you to halt to unhealthy hurt, anger, and jealousy.

Acquiring Self-Acceptance

All human beings are equal in worth. Just stop and ponder on how much you tend to agree with that statement. Isn't human life sacred? Isn't it the reason as to why murder is a criminal offense regardless of who is killed? Most of us learned that human beings have intrinsic worth and value (this means that we are worthy and valuable just by the fact that we exist). But then we often behave as if some individuals are more worthy and valuable than others. We normally attach too much significance to certain things such as social status and wealth. One might erroneously assume that individuals who possess these traits or conditions are superior to others or who lack them. Altogether, you may still undervalue or attach too little importance to features of your personhood such as kindness, generosity, and social responsibility.

Making comparisons between oneself and others based on external factors or conditions leads one to feel inferior or superior, in turns. Both positions are not healthy as one puts down himself or others. Finding/acquiring self-acceptance means that one can identify that we are all equal in worth though may be unequal in other factors. Thus, one may be a poor driver and an exceptional cook while his friend may be the exact opposite. They are still both worthy persons but have totally different limitations and strengths. One of the first key steps towards self-acceptance is taking note of conditions to which you characteristically attach your self-worth.

Accepting and Improving Yourself at the Same Time

Perhaps one is likely to think that accepting yourself denotes that they can surrender self-improvement and let oneself off the hook to any wicked actions he/she may be involved in or neglect good actions. We do not hope so, as that is not our message to you. Taking everything into account, if you accept yourself as basically worthwhile given your bad behaviors or shortcomings, you are in a better position to work on them than if you judge and condemn yourself. We recommend that you instantaneously give yourself some room to be less perfect and continue striving to make personal vital changes. This can be a technique for self-improvement success. The best way is by picking extremely specific areas for self-improvement If you desire to improve your conduct and life in general. By saying 'I want to be a better person' might be true but it does not give adequate information to get on with. The exact detail is what matters.

When you appropriately be responsible for your behavior as well as your emotions you are much more likely to make efficient changes. Blaming others or life event/conditions for your troubled emotions or self-destructive behavior, you are giving up your power to better up things. Self-acceptance requires a lot of practice. At times you are likely to find that confidence and doing as per your new attitudes may be easy and sometimes doing so may be more difficult.

Maintaining Relationships

Your ability to get along with others depends on your ability to be accepting of them and to experience healthy negative emotions instead of unhealthy ones such as rage, hate, and fury. Unhealthy anger is a common reason for relationship problems. Another common cause of interpersonal difficulties is low self-opinion. In this chapter, we help you to work out what type of anger you most often experience and to get better at being healthily angry. We also give you a few exercises to strengthen your acceptance of yourself and others – thereby increasing your chances of developing satisfying and functional relationships.

Overcoming Outrage

Everyone, from time to time, becomes angry, loses their temper, throws a wobbly, blows their top, and goes berserk. Though some behave in this way more frequently than others. Losing your temper may cause glitches in your friendships, romantic life, family relationships, as well as work life. Identifying whether the type of feelings you are experiencing unhealthy outrage or not is the first key step in overcoming the depression. Overcoming outrage is a key step in overcoming depression as anger usually leads to depression in most cases. Hence the need for us to help you understand the difference between appropriate annoyance and irrational rage

1. Recognizing healthy anger

Let us look at the features of healthy annoyance. When one is healthily angry, he or she tends to think in a balanced manner and accepts way about other people. One tends to identify that another person stepped on his toe or violated one of his rules without deciding that he or she really should have note done so. the person still tends to feel in control of himself and behaves in a mad but non-threatening manner.

2. Seeing aspects of unhealthy anger

Unhealthy anger is characterized by specific ways of acting, thinking as well as certain physical feelings. Unhealthy anger denotes that you are thinking in harsh ways regarding others and acting in an intimidating way. The sensation typically feels very uncomfortable and overwhelming. Unhealthy anger, as a rule, lasts for long and is more strongly uncomfortable as compared to the healthier version.

3. Counting the Cost of being Angry

Being unhealthily angry has major negative consequences on one's relationships as well as life in general. At times one might think that their fury has useful benefits that healthy anger would not bring about. You are doubtless wrong. Normally, you are clearer and more efficient at putting across points if you are not mad with hostility.

4. Lengthening Your Fuse

At this point, you might be having a feeling that you mostly feel like having unhealthily anger and that it has had some negative effects and outcome on you. So, what's next? Handling your anger can be challenging, nevertheless, if you decide and are ready to you will need to put in some serious effort, you can do it. In case you have stern rules which you always command others to adhere to, then you are susceptible to unhealthily anger when they break your rules. Granting others, the opportunity to speak out their opinion is a key step towards encountering healthy anger. As well, having a preference for how others ought to behave but not demanding that everyone else do as per your wish helps you to evade unhealthy outrage.

5. Embracing Effective Assertion

For one to learn properly on how to be assertive they need to do a lot of practice, so permit yourself to get it wrong a few times before getting it right. The best way to become assertive is to accept that both you and the other person are imperfect human beings who can make errors and mistakes. Then listen to other people and think about what you want to give as a response. This process is very relevant if you are amidst a huge disagreement or you are the recipient of critical remarks. Healthy assertion regards getting your point across as well as defending your rights when other people are treating you poorly and unfairly. Unlike aggression, assertion does not mean demonstrating to others that you are right, and they are wrong. An assertion is aimed at being a civil exchange to resolve differences as well as reach a concession. When you are being assertive you are inclined to do the following things:

- Refraining from any threat of violence or violence itself.

- Avoiding intimidating, diminishing, unduly upsetting others

- Speaking respectfully to others without using abusive, offensive language or name-calling.

- Allowing others to speak their minds and express their views.

- Engaging in discussions with others rather than trying to win an argument.

- Striving to sort out the differences where possible or rather agree to disagree on a point. When settling a disagreement, you may need to look for an environment that is private enough to converse from when both parties have time.

Always remember that conditions do not have to be faultless for you to discuss differences with another person, though it aids in reducing possible distractions. If it is a work difference, you might have to book an appointment with your colleague or boss to speak to have a better conversation.

Putting Yourself at Par with Your Peers

Low self-confidence can cause all kinds of social difficulties. As described earlier on, seeing yourself in this manner bring about unhealthy anger. It can as well cause you to compare yourself harshly and negatively with others. You may feel socially nervous as you essentially believe that others will not like you or even accept you just as you are. Among the best methods for you to really appreciate social interaction, maintain relationships, and make friends is to view yourself equal to all others in human worth. Having this perspective may seem to be quite easy, but like many CBT values, practicing it may be considerably harder. One's sense of equality entails surrendering your need to be more superior so as not to feel inferior. As well it entails being your real self and letting others to like or dislike based on that– and vice versa. Viewing yourself equal to others includes accepting, embracing, and even rejoicing in your own ordinariness.

Conclusion

Now you have reached the end of this book, but not the end of your CBT journey. These pages have prepared you to use CBT to transform your mind and consequently your life. That does not mean that your journey is over; rather, it has just begun. CBT is your best friend. It is a companion that you should carry with you through the rest of your life. Keep using it to see marked changes in how you approach life and how you feel.

Here is a wrap up of everything covered in this book:

Avoiding situations that bring you harm is great. But in real life, we both know that that is not always realistic. Life throws plenty of bad situations at you and you can't avoid them all. Therefore, it is essential to develop healthy coping skills for when you do encounter these situations.

Situations that stir up mental illness symptoms can be everyday situations that other, healthier people find to be no big deal. But for you, they can feel catastrophic. They can lead you to relapse in your symptoms, after working so hard to overcome those symptoms with CBT. Learning to cope in harmful everyday situations is essential to keep yourself from falling into despair.

Anxiety

Many everyday situations that are nothing to healthy people can trigger severe anxiety in some. For instance, a huge crowd at an airport can be stressful for anyone, but it can be disastrous for you if you have agoraphobia or social anxiety. But what if you have to fly for work or to visit a sick relative? You have to be a part of that airport crowd, whether you like it or not. The situation is not ideal for you but you can use various techniques to cope with your anxiety.

The best technique is relaxation. Focus on your breathing. Breathe in through your nose, out through your mouth. By focusing on your breathing, you take your mind off of the stress that surrounds it.

Progressive muscle relaxation also is helpful in anxiety-provoking situations. Start first from the muscles in your scalp. Force yourself to relax those muscles. Next move to your forehead muscles. Keep roving your mind over your body, forcing the relaxation of each of your muscle groups. The relaxation will calm you and the intense mental focus required to perform this exercise will take your mind off of your stress.

Some people find tapping to be soothing. You can repeat a mantra to yourself such as, "I will survive this. This is really not so bad" as you tap different parts of your body. The physical action of tapping paired with the repeated affirmation can help trick your mind into believing what you are saying to yourself.

Sometimes anxiety can impair your ability to focus on anything. In that case, it is essential to pick a spot on the wall and focus on it intently. Do not chase any other thoughts that enter your head. That spot on the wall is your refuge. Use it to take your mind off of the craziness raging around you and within you.

Facing Your Fears

CBT is great for helping you overcome irrational fears and phobias. This is because CBT allows you to think about your phobias and understand that they are not rational and not conducive to your peace of mind.

If you have a phobia, you may find it very helpful to write about your phobia. When it is on paper, you will begin to see how silly it really is. If you are scared of airplanes, what are the odds of a crash, really? You are far more likely to die in a car crash than a plane crash.

If you are scared of dogs because of a traumatic encounter with a dog in your childhood, remember that most dogs are man's best friends and that you are a lot bigger now. Analyze your fears to see how scary they really are.

To truly overcome your phobia, you need to begin to condition yourself to it. Exposing yourself to what scares you can help teach your mind to stop fearing it as it witnesses you emerge unscathed. There are classes you can take to condition yourself to overcome fear of heights, flying, and other phobias. Consider going to the snake or spider exhibit at a local zoo to stand near the creatures that make you want to scream. You will begin to realize that your phobias do not hurt you. If you have social phobia, try taking brief walks outside and striking up a brief conversation with one stranger a day.

The above relaxation techniques can also really help you when you are feeling the vise grip of fear from a phobia. Breathe, focus, and use progressive muscle relaxation to bring yourself out of your fear.

Handling Depression

The hardest part of coping with depression is that depression cripples your will to do anything. You may not even have the energy to get out of bed, let alone perform CBT on yourself. But coping with your depression gets easier when you begin to change your thinking to more positive thoughts. Positive thinking has the ability to release feel-good hormones like serotonin in your brain, allowing you to feel better and begin to move forward with your life.

When you find yourself drowning in depression symptoms, there may be a reason that you feel so blue. Maybe life is just hard right now or you have not been taking care of your body. Try to identify the source of your depression and remove it from your life. Focus on the present and enjoying life right now. Life is too short to be spent suffering in your bed.

Anger Management

If you have trouble managing your anger, you need to step back and breathe when you start to see red. Use your CBT journal to write down why a situation made you mad enough to hit someone or have an outburst. Then, analyze the situation. Was it really what you thought, or were you doing something like assuming and negative labeling? Were you ignoring the positives of the situation, or of a person that angered you? Now, in the future, how can you handle this situation without hitting and throwing things and lashing out verbally? Is there something you can do that is more conducive to a reasonable solution?

Rarely is anger ever a solution. Uncontrolled anger can get you into a lot of trouble with loved ones and even the law. Breathe, and think of better ways to react to situations than angry outbursts.

Using CBT to Overcome addiction

Addiction is often referred to as an illness. Many people fail to understand that addiction is usually a symptom of a deeper illness. People use drugs, alcohol, and other addictive behaviors such as gambling to create instant gratification and numb themselves against life. These addictive behaviors offer addicts temporary pleasure that drowns out the deeper pain addicts are experiencing inside of themselves. Basically, addicts use their addictions to distract themselves, or numb themselves, from what is really wrong. When the pleasure wears off, addicts literally feel like they are in hell because they have no shield from their pain, and they desperately chase a new high or thrill to keep them in the numb, pleased state that lets them ignore their problems. Addicts often live in denial of their real problems, and engage in harmful behaviors to avoid feeling the emotional fallout from their life situations, past traumas, or their childhoods.

Since CBT can address inner thoughts and thus change outer behaviors, it offers a rich opportunity for addicts to overcome their addictions. Addicts can use CBT to identify the thoughts and emotions that drive them to use and replace those thoughts and emotions with healthier ones that do not drive them to seek numbness. It also helps them learn to avoid situations, also known as triggers, which lead to relapses. In addition, addicts can use CBT to find healthy alternatives to self-medicating using substances, shopping, gambling, eating, sex, or whatever vice they have chosen to escape their problems with.

Identify addictive behaviors and the thoughts behind them. If you suddenly crave a drug, what triggered you to want to use? Was it a tense situation, like an argument with your family or a rough day at work? Did you see someone or hear a song from your drug days that made your brain start thinking about drugs?

Now, think of better ways to cope with the current situation. Maybe you can do yoga or exercise to relieve stress. Maybe just writing in your journal and taking a hot shower is all you need. Engage in healthy feel-good coping mechanisms, rather than participating in substance use. While substance use can relieve your bad feelings in the short term, it only worsens your mental health and your life circumstances in the long term.

Above all, remember your resolve to be clean and sober. You have made tremendous progress. Your life and your health are probably significantly better without drugs and alcohol playing a role in your behavior. You don't want to backtrack now and discount everything that you have accomplished. One way to deal with cravings and addiction is to remember why you wanted to get clean in the first place.

Remind yourself of the awful things about drug use that made you want to quit.

Then, think about all that you have accomplished in getting clean. You have done something that less than fourteen percent of drug users do.

SELF ESTEEM AND SELF CONFIDENCE

THE BEGINNERS GUIDE TO BUILD AND MANAGE RELATIONSHIPS. UNDERSTAND OTHERS, INCREASE YOUR CONFIDENCE AND IMPROVE YOUR SOCIAL SKILLS FOR A HAPPIER LIFE.

Table of Contents

Introduction

Let me clue you in on a secret. This is a secret because a lot of people don't like to admit this. The secret is most people are unsure; most people lack confidence. Now, don't get too excited. Lacking confidence does not necessarily mean that they have absolutely no self-confidence. They lack enough confidence. In other words, it's below the level that they need to live their lives at peak performance.

Now, this revelation is actually quite apparent. You just examine all the lives of people you know, and I can guarantee you that 80% of the time, they are living below their fullest potential. In other words, they are capable of so much more yet they settle for a life that is several levels below that full potential. They're settling; they're taking second place. They're not venturing forth to the fullest extent of what they are capable of getting out of life.

Again, the reason for this is that they lack confidence. They are not confident enough. This is why people who possess self-confidence at high levels are very magnetic. People who lack confidence are drawn to confident people. Now, don't get too excited. It's easy to see the positive aspect of this; it's very easy to see people who are drawn to you, and they encourage you. The bottom line, whether they say it or not, is that I'm drawn to you because you have something that I don't have at a high enough level.

However, you can also draw people in the wrong ways. There are people who lack confidence, and they know it, so they try to attack, expose, or put on the spot people who are obviously more confident than them. There is always that variation.

The bottom line is that in whatever form it takes, confident people are "magnetic" precisely because they make people around them feel comfortable. Again, there is negative magnetism because people who are envious of what you have. They want to be comfortable, but they feel they have to attack you because they feel that's the only way they can make up for their own lack of confidence.

Regardless, when you're confident, you're automatically magnetic. Confident people fulfil other people's perception or wish for comfort and support. In other words, people around you are looking for leadership. They're like lost sheep looking for a shepherd. I know that sounds insulting because when you say to someone's face that he is acting like a sheep, don't be surprised if you get a fist in your mouth.

But that's the truth, people at some level or another, lack enough confidence, and they know this. This is why they naturally gravitate towards people with a healthy level of easily visible and easily detected self-confidence. Why does this happen? Why are people looking for leadership? Well, confident people make those around them feel things are possible. This is the mark of leadership. When you make people around you feel that certain things are possible, they can't get enough of you. Why? Left to their own devices or left to themselves, they feel things are harder than they really are. They feel that things are not easy and that there are many obstacles along the way.

When you come around and inspire them, and they feel that things are possible, they can't help but sit up and pay attention. You make them feel the certain things that they can't normally feel on their own. If you hang around long enough confident people, they get others to feel that things are not only possible, but probable. This is what people are looking for in leadership. This is what people are looking for in their social circles.

Have you ever noticed groups of teenagers and that some of them are more aggressive than others? Well, when you take a group of teenage boys, who are otherwise usually timid, and throw in there a leader of the same age who motivates them to do certain things, you'd be surprised as to what that group can do. Of course, this can play out either positively or negatively.

A lot of the hooligan violence and gang violence that you hear about in the news usually involve groups of teenagers that have a leader or two that push them to feel that certain things are not only possible, but probable. Rob a liquor store? Well, if the leader is not in the mix, then that's just an idle fantasy. Once you throw in the right person in their midst, it's only a matter of time until the group knocks over a liquor store.

You see how this works? This can play out positively or negatively. But the truth cannot be denied that confident people get others around them to feel that things are not only possible but probable. I don't know about you, but that is the definition of power.

The Bottom Line

Confident people can create a "personal reality field" around themselves. It's easy for you to walk around and think that certain things are possible, and certain things are not possible. Everybody is entitled to that. However, the moment you come across somebody who is very confident, it's very easy for you to fall under their influence. It's very easy for you to believe that they're persuasive.

Now, their answers to the questions you're confronting may not be all that better than your answers, but it wouldn't feel like it. Why? Their level of self-confidence is so infectious that it persuades you to think that if this person seems so gung-ho about what they're saying, it must be true. You might be absolutely correct in your conclusion because you're thinking might be based on logic and reason and past experiences, but all of that goes out the window. Instead, you're just blown away by this person's confidence, and you allow that factor to persuade you to come to an opposite conclusion.

Confident people also create a personal reality field around them through group cohesion. Believe it or not, when two or more people hang out in the same group, and they start repeating certain things, they start hypnotizing each other. They start persuading each other to think that ideas that they individually have a problem with are true. There is such a thing as group thinks, and the cause of such group cohesion is, you guessed it, confident people.

Once this happens, confident people can marshal the individual strengths and competencies of the group towards common goals. This is the essence of leadership. What's important to understand here is that just because you're able to do this because of your natural confidence, it doesn't automatically mean that you will have formal leadership roles, at least in the beginning. In other words, just because you are able to do this, don't think that your boss will automatically say, "Okay, you're promoted." It sometimes takes a while; there is such a thing as office politics after all.

However, the place that you work for would be stupid to overlook your organic leadership because whether people have fancy titles or occupy high places in the hierarchy chart, their natural leadership isn't undeniable. It really is the organization's loss to continue to turn a blind eye to the organic leadership of certain individuals in the organization. I need you to keep this in mind because it's easy to think of self-confidence as something that would be "nice to have." No, it's not an option.

If you want to go anywhere in life, if you want to live up to your fullest potential, if you want to stop living a life of frustration and disappointment, you need to invest time, effort and energy in building up your self-confidence, and it will turn you into an organic leader who will, sooner or later, turn into a formal leadership role.

Chapter 1 What is Self Esteem?

The world of the self is full of different characteristics and textures. You must have heard the phrase 'self-esteem' being mentioned by prominent psychologists and experts quite a lot. Such is the importance of this phrase that from workplace motivational speeches to the session you have with your psychologist, it is mentioned everywhere in abundance.

So, knowing that you have encountered this word countless times before, we expect you to wonder what exactly self-esteem is. We know the meaning of both these words on their own, but how do you define them when both these words are combined to form one phrase.

As we already know, this book is going to do wonders for your self-esteem and the self-esteem of others around you. You can use this book to improve how you feel about yourself. But, before we can start talking about self-esteem and doing something about your self-esteem, you need to understand the concept of this word and how it came out to be as important as it is the world of psychology and motivation as it is today.

The basics of self-esteem can be understood by understanding the characteristics of people who have high self-esteem. High self-esteem can be said to be an abundance of respect and esteem for oneself in your mind.

People with high self-esteem are more often than not good friends with themselves. They enjoy their own company and accept themselves for who they are. They look after themselves and hold no bars in befriending their minds. You may know someone who looks after themselves, is intrinsically motivated and also happens to be quite a charmer when it comes to talking with other people. That someone probably has a good self-esteem, because they value themselves for who or what they are and do not mind talking to other people based on the face value that they have achieved over time. People with high self-esteem often happen to be intrinsically motivated as well.

If your biggest friend is present within you, you do not have to look at the outside world for motivation to do stuff. The biggest motivator present within you can help intrinsically motivate you to do stuff that you never imagined you would do. People with high self-esteem also offer amazing company. They can talk at ends about anything concerning life or them and do not hold any bars when it comes to expressing their desires.

On the other hand, we also expect you to know people or women who don't take care of themselves and don't have a heightened or realistic opinion of their abilities. They undermine their abilities, run into a lot of comparisons and do not actually realize how talented they are. In short, the kind of person we are talking of here would look in the mirror and hate themselves. Now, low self-esteem does not come down to ground facts or realities. Someone with low self-esteem could be the most beautiful woman alive with charming skin and whatnot, but their low self-esteem would prompt them into hating what they see in the mirror. Their bodies would never satisfy them, and they would almost always remain unfulfilled or unsatisfied with what they have given by good. It is believed that people with low self-esteem never end up achieving their true potential or what they truly can because they never realize all the talents that are hidden inside of them.

Definitions for Self-Esteem

Psychologists that have studied the concept of self-esteem have come up with different examples to define it to the average human. These definitions shed new light on the concept of self-esteem and just shine upon us the importance that it hosts. A low self-esteem can have different repercussions and high self-esteem can have different benefits, these definitions define how you can benefit or lose out through the levels of self-esteem you have.

The first definition of self-esteem we are studying was first proposed by Glenn Schiraldi as part of the Self-Esteem Workbook. This definition has much to do with the appreciation a person has for themselves. Schiraldi believed that self-esteem was all about having a realistic and appreciative opinion of yourself. The opinion should be realistic because as important as it is to not undermine your abilities, you shouldn't also have high expectations of what you consider yourself capable to do.

Having high expectations from oneself can be a bit too risky, as you can end up disappointing yourself and the people around you. Schiraldi believed that the opinion of oneself should be appreciative because that is exactly what goes on to define the self-esteem that people have in them. Self-esteem is all about appreciating the things you do and building upon them to keep repeating the success that you achieve. You surely cannot work towards success in the best manner possible, without appreciating your talents and working towards further bettering them. Schiraldi used the word appreciative to imply that you should have positive feelings and optimism towards yourself and should have a certain bit of liking towards your abilities as well.

The second definition we study was proposed by renowned psychologist David Burns. Burns positioned self-esteem at an extremely high pedestal, because of how he believed it could influence the human body and mind. Burns was himself a prominent psychologist and had worked with multiple individuals before he came up with this understanding. Burns realized that self-esteem was one of the most important factors helping people towards achieving the success they craved in life. It is said that believes and evaluations you hold about yourself will go on to determine what you become in your life. You cannot seriously have zero belief in yourself and expect good results to come by. To make sure that you achieve success, you should have full belief in your abilities and should focus on the end goal that you have in your mind.

The third definition of self-esteem that we study was proposed by Stanley Coopersmith. Coopersmith was another prominent psychologist and knew a fair deal about self-esteem and how it could motivate people into achieving the goals that they have in mind. Coopersmith was good at the art of psychology and mentioned that humans can use their self-esteem for their good. Coopersmith mentioned that the self-esteem you have is basically a personal judgment or analysis for expressing your worthiness towards your attitude. According to him, your self-esteem is an attitude that you show based on the worthiness that you hold about yourself. The attitude can turn deplorable if you don't consider yourself worthy enough, while the same attitude can turn into a benefit for you if you go on to achieve what comes with it.

These three are the major definitions that we have seen concerning self-esteem in the world of psychology. These definitions define self-esteem to us and put into perspective three different facets or faces of how self-esteem can be looked at.

Now is a time for a bit of self-reflection to absorb what you have just studied. Your internal self-esteem is all about understanding your flaws and working on them to better them. You should look to better your flaws by understanding your self-esteem and what comes within it.

The following questions will help you in self-reflecting in an advisable manner and achieving the results we would want you to achieve through this process.

• What have you noticed about self-esteem through the definitions above? Do you think that the definitions are in line with the judgments or the perception you had about self-esteem back in the day?

• Do these definitions we have studied differ from the definitions you had in mind related to the self-esteem of a human? If they do differ, do you think the difference is a minute one or something that you should study in detail?

• Based on all your ideas and definitions of self-esteem and the explanations you have just read; how would you define self-esteem in your words? What does self-esteem mean to you, in your own words?

• Do you think that you have a stable self-esteem, or is it fluctuating all the time? People often think they have multiple self-esteems, based on how their mood is. A positive mood can lead to optimism and high self-esteem, while a negative mood can more often than not lead to dwindling self-esteem, where you don't happen to have a lot of ideas about what you are doing with your life and pessimism creeps over you.

Healthy Self-Esteem

Your self-esteem can become healthy for you if it is developed and crafted the right way. Before we go on rambling about the benefits of healthy self-esteem, we first need to discuss what a healthy self-esteem is.

A healthy self-esteem is something that happens when a person values themselves and likes themselves for who they are. The idea of healthy self-esteem comes with the idea that you are a worthy being and have some kind of role to play in how this universe works. A healthy self-esteem includes realizing that humans are fallible and have different characteristics. Humans make mistakes; in fact, making mistakes is what makes you human. You need to realize that there is no harm in erring at one time or the other. Everyone makes mistakes and you to make certain mistakes in your life. A person with a healthy self-esteem happens to be their own best friend, which is why they realize that making mistakes does not necessarily make them a bad person. It just makes them human.

People with low self-esteem take making mistakes as a sign of their uselessness. Every single mistake they make is followed by sessions of over-thinking where they dissect the mistake and hate themselves further for erring in judgment. The end conclusion after these hours of thinking is that they happen to be useless and bad for making that small mistake.

A person with a healthy self-esteem realizes that making mistakes is not a crime. And, they also realize how important it is for them to be their own best friend. Befriending yourself is part of a healthy self-esteem. When you befriend yourself, you realize that you can err. You can make errors. And, when you realize that you can make errors, you also realize how to keep loving yourself throughout these errors. A person with a healthy self-esteem has high regard and self-respect, just as you would do for a friend, only that the regard and love are now used for oneself.

People with high self-esteem do not like degrading themselves when talking to someone else. They realize that the conversation is temporary and that their love and friendship with their bodies would continue for the time to come. People who don't have a healthy self-esteem degrade and pull jokes on themselves in a conversation. These jokes end up ruining their self-confidence in the long run.

Self-esteem is an important part of our life based on how much it affects us. Self-esteem is the filter through which we react to everything that we are experiencing and everything that happens to us. You can let your low self-esteem get to your mind or can work on it to improve it and make it healthy for your future success. Remember that the first pre-requisite of building healthy self-esteem is to love yourself and befriend yourself.

Why Is Self-Esteem Important?

While we have listed down the different definitions of self-esteem and the healthy aspect related to having good self-esteem, it is now time to shed some light on the importance of self-esteem.

By now, you must also be wondering about the importance of self-esteem in the context of our lives. Having high self-esteem is increasingly healthy and important for you because of the benefits it hosts and how it saves you from the downsides of having low self-esteem.

People with low self-esteem happen to have numerous mental and physical repercussions as a result of their attitude. People who have low self-esteem can develop mental illnesses such as anxiety and depression as part of this attitude. Mental illnesses and problems usually start when a person doesn't value themselves and the value they add to this world.

You are the best version of yourself and nobody else can top that. The sooner you realize this the better it is for you. People who have a hard time appreciating themselves for who they are and what they do, happen to live life within their bubble of low self-esteem. The issues begin when you first start questioning something related to you; something natural. It could be your height, your physical characteristics or your voice. You start wishful thinking and hope that you can rid yourself of that certain characteristic. That is when you enter an area of no return and start delving into the subjugated world of wishful thinking. Positive self-esteem, on the flip side, includes accepting yourself for who you are. You accept yourself for what you bring to the table and don't want it to be any different.

Once you start undervaluing yourself, you would start seeing a fall in the performance that you would want to give around you. A wide range of problems take birth when you start undervaluing yourself. These problems include negative thinking, disordered eating habits, abuse, unhealthy relationship pattern, poor body image, underachievement in professional or academic life and impaired communication skills.

The image you have of yourself is what can save you from falling deep into the pits of what we have mentioned or talked about above. You can consider your self-esteem as the roots of the tree of life. Your roots define how hard or balanced you stand in your life. If your roots are based on a weakened and flawed sense of self, then you will never be able to grow to the limits you have in mind. Stunted mental growth is also a result of low self-esteem; you never achieve the kind of mental growth you want. Albeit, when you base your life on a positive self-esteem, you make sure that your roots remain firm and resilient. While low self-esteem can fluster and shaken you, high self-esteem can save you from complete annihilation or failure in life.

Difference between Self-Confidence and Self-Esteem

You must have gone through the lines above and must be thinking that self-esteem is a lot like the definition of self-confidence you have in your mind. There are some minute but distinguishable differences between the concept of self-confidence and self-esteem. These concepts indulge in the ability or worthiness of your mind, but they have a greater meaning attached to them.

Self-confidence is the confidence or the judgment that you have in your abilities. You know you can do something, but how confident you are about that thing defines your self-confidence. You can have a lot of confidence in some areas of life but can lack confidence in other areas of life. For instance, a student might think that they are very good at debating, but poor at sports. Now, when they enter the debating arena their confidence might be sky high and their oomph will be completely different. But, when they enter the sports field, all the self-confidence will fall down and they will be back to ground one. For instance, the same student can have a lot of confidence while handling math but could lack that confidence in spellings. See, you can have confidence in some of your abilities while lack of confidence in the other abilities at the same time. While you still may be confident about some abilities, you can generally be categorized for having low self-esteem because of your attitude to your worthiness.

Moving on, our confidence in our abilities is something that fluctuates. As we have illustrated and defined above, you can have different levels of confidence in different abilities. The level of confidence in a particular ability could be based on how confident you feel when doing that activity. On the contrary, self-esteem tends to be a more constant figure. Your self-esteem while doing Task A would be the same as your self-esteem for doing Task B. When it comes to self-esteem, you're thinking of yourself as a whole figure, you're not just taking one or two abilities into perspective. Once you think yourself as a whole, your confidence in a couple of activities makes no difference. If your general attitude to your worthiness isn't anything to write home about, then you will generally be considered low on self-esteem.

Additionally, we can also say that self-confidence is an easier attribute or attitude to build than self-esteem. While you can also build your self-esteem, as we will expertly show within this book, you cannot seriously manage your self-esteem in the same manner as your self-confidence. All it takes to build your self-confidence in a particular ability is to practice it, again and again, hoping that you will make certain improvements. But, with self-esteem, you have to change your greater outlook to life. There is a certain amount of inter-play as well between both the concepts of self-esteem and self-confidence. It is usually believed that someone with low self-esteem will most definitely have low self-confidence while doing most of the tasks. Your self-confidence in your tasks is based on your actual ability to do that task and your perception of that ability. While you might be fully able to do something, your low self-esteem can push your confidence for doing that particular task down. However, most people with low self-esteem happen to have a couple of tasks or activities where their self-confidence can rocket to the sky. Keeping this in mind, the concept of self-confidence is treated separately to that of self-esteem.

Chapter 2 Understanding Self Confidence

When a person displays a certain level of self-confidence this indicates that he or she has a positive outlook towards him or herself as well as demonstrating a heightened sense of certainty related to what he or she can do in terms of the skill sets that come easily or easier than other sets of skills that he or she might have. That being said, this definition is very simplistic and broad as while it is clear that any person who is confident in him or herself believes that he or she can meet certain goals that they have been working towards for a specific period of time as well as the notion that he or she displays a strong sense of adoration for the kind of person that he or she happens to be, there is a lot more to having self-confidence that goes beyond these very principles. At this point, you might have come to the belief that any person who indicates or clearly demonstrates that he or she has a high level of confidence in him or herself is considered to be a separate category connected to the various types of people that exist in the world. However, this is not necessarily the case as the cognitive patterns that influence the view that a person has towards him, or herself is the factor that determines whether he or she is self-confident or not, thus in other words, the people who harbor the cognitive patterns that influence them into believing that they are in fact decent human beings that can do anything that they put their minds to have self-confidence not because of self-confidence being an innate trait that is exhibited by certain individuals, to begin with. When a person displays self-confidence they are able to lead a life where they are confronted with circumstances that are rather pleasing and enable them to prosper in the long run as a direct consequence, which means that the people who are able to share the consensus that they are naturally satisfied with the kind of person that they are, then they are otherwise all the more capable of coming to conclusion that they can be pleasantly tolerant of themselves and project a more general vivacious attitude as well. In addition, those who are equipped with a more prevalent form of self-confidence will find that they are more likely to exude a focus on acquiring exactly what they are trying to obtain, to begin with, such as the things that a person has fantasized about obtaining for a certain amount of time or acquiring whatever it is that intrigues him or her and once this occurs these kinds of people are able to gain prosperity as an end result.

However, the notion of self-confidence goes well beyond cognitive processes, for people are able to depend on their own confidence in who they are as individuals without having to rely on the encouragement that comes from the people who formulate their close-knit intimate social circle, and it does not have to only be depended on from more intense and difficult events. Some of these various difficult events include but are not limited to life throwing a curveball that deprives you of the financial assets that you counted on to determine the quantity of prosperity that you have gained over time and realizing that the people that you thought you could trust were not so reliable either you can still find that having confidence in yourself proves to be quite valuable as it can help you rediscover the full extent of your overall worth to help you work through these extremely painful sudden circumstances. While it accurate to label the confidence that one has towards him or herself to be an organic element of the essence of their being even if it is not something that a person is born with, this does not suggest in any way that the only way for a person to develop any belief in what they can do, and the positive attitude that they cultivate towards themselves is from the influence of those who are important and vital to their existence in terms of being their respective loved ones or from something that does not organically comprise of your being. This stems from the principle, as you may have already guessed, known as the very things that you as a person have proved to yourself as well as to other people that you can, in fact, perform in an excellent capacity without bothering to let the lingering critical and or judgmental remarks that are recited by people who are prevalent in your life. Moreover, these are not just something that you are equipped with for all people are blessed with the same ability to hold a positive view of yourself and the kinds of skills and activities that you are able to do well as opposed to having a more negative view of yourself and the kinds of skills that you are able to do well. Furthermore, along with everyone else, you are equipped with a sense of worth that is most certainly worth recognizing and that the skill sets that you can perform at an excellent level are crucial assets, despite the fact that there are people out there who will actively try to question this and come to the conviction that these attitudes that you have towards yourself do not hold any sufficient merit, as well as holding a more favorable attitude towards who you are as a person despite all of the possible obstacles and curveballs that life can throw at you. Of course, this simply suggests that a person who is able to help foster his or her belief in what they can actually do as well as remain pleased and accepting of the kind of person that he or she happens to be is able to consistently stimulate a more heightened presence of such notions within their overall character or that a person may use these as guides to helping them to develop more confidence in themselves over time, if such a person does not view their self in a more favorably way nor does he or she already view him or herself through a more positive lens.

At this point you probably think that a lot of this information is just reiterations of a previously made point and a collection of redundant insights that simple highlight the idea that in order to have self-confidence you have to be exceptionally positive all the time and constantly harbor the belief that you can do and perform all the skills you have mastered with excellence, which is completely understandable and valid. Yet, I would like to remind you that while this might seem rather repetitive, the sole objective of this chapter is to provide a more general comprehension of what self-confidence is, before delving into how you can improve the level of self-confidence that you have as well as the numerous theories that focus on the analysis of the self-confidence found within a specific person. Furthermore, life will push you to fight the criticism that other people can display at you, whether or not it is intentionally malicious or not, such as when you are forced to contend with reciting a presentation that shall be viewed by a wide horde of spectators who are perhaps not exactly receptive to engaging and actively listening to what you have to offer. If you are someone who nonetheless believes that you can recite an amazing performance than this will help to drown out the unpleasant distractions that are being displayed at your own expense by the people who are observing the presentation that you are currently giving instead of causing you to succumb to their judgmental statements and to no longer believe that you are indeed capable of performing a decent presentation, to begin with. As a result, once you have been able to realize that you can do a presentation of high quality despite the objections recited by those who are witnessing you perform this in front of them you can use the objections that other people have made towards you while you were reciting this presentation in order to hone and to further develop the presentation skill set that you have mastered which will help to inspire you to believe in yourself even more which will most certainly come in handy once you have to emerge in front of a crowd and give some sort of presentation.

The opposite way to demonstrate self-confidence is to a demonstrate a lack of belief in what you are capable of doing to the point where it proves to be detrimental to your mental well-being, for you only think highly of yourself until you are confronted with a remark that criticizes your ability to perform a certain task. Thus, in order to change this, you must be willing to obtain new knowledge about what it takes to be more confident in yourself and following the specific guides that shall help this belief in yourself to continue to grow within you. By now, you must be curious as to what are the various kinds of theories that comprise this topic, which will be covered further during the next chapter.

What Confidence is All About?

Hello there! I would like to congratulate you for taking your first step towards becoming a more confident person. You will be glad to know that this adventure will change your life forever.

The Definition of Confidence

Confidence is believing in your ability to make the right decision and take the right steps in a given situation, no matter how difficult or easy it seems to be.

Of course, by having the confidence to overcome life's challenges, there is nothing wrong with feeling good about it. You can even think of it as a positive side effect.

How to Measure your Level of Confidence

If you want to know your current level of confidence, perhaps you would like to take this short test. It will be a great idea to write down your responses in a journal. That way, you can take a look at it later on in the future and see how you have developed since then.

Before you begin, keep in mind that there is no such thing as a right or wrong response. Be honest with yourself as you can then reveal the aspects of your life with an impact on your self-confidence.

Now, keep in mind the following scale:

Strongly Agree: SA

Agree: A

Neutral: N

Disagree: D

Strongly Disagree: SD

Write down your response using this guide as you go through each of the following statements:

I know exactly how I want to live my life.

I know my values clearly.

I have chosen a purpose in my life and I am working towards it.

I can take a step back to assess my thoughts and emotions during a stressful situation.

I do not remind myself constantly of my failures.

I have a reputation of being an optimist.

I spend most of my time doing the things that I love.

I occasionally find myself being incredibly focused on a task.

I value myself and the people around me.

    I am fully aware of both my strengths and flaws.

    I know what other people see in me.

I have no problems with getting into the details and looking at the bigger picture at the same time.

I sometimes seek advice from the people I trust when I have decisions to make.

I love experiencing new things and I see challenges as an opportunity to grow.

I enjoy learning a new skill and opening up to different perspectives.

I am willing to take risks in a healthy way.

I consider myself as healthy because I take care of my body.

I always find time to rest and relax each day.

I believe that progress, no matter how small, is better than perfection.

I occasionally spend time to concentrate deeply and connect with the different facets of myself.

After responding to each statement, the next step is to score yourself.

For each "SA" give yourself 5 points.

For each "A" give yourself 4 points.

For each "N" give yourself 3 points.

For each "D" give yourself 2 points.

For each "SD" give yourself 1 point.

Once you have given yourself the appropriate points for each statement, total your score and compare it with the following rating scale:

If you scored between an 80 and 100:

Overall, you are what others consider as a confident person. You know exactly who you are and what you stand for, and you are currently working towards achieving your goals and purpose in life.

If you scored between a 60 and 79:

You are fairly confident most of the time. There are certain times in your life when you feel challenged, but you know how to manage them by seeking help. You even picked up this book to help you work towards becoming more confident, so good for you!

If you scored between a 40 and 59:

You may be experiencing some doubts in your life as of the moment, and you may be wondering what to do next. Don't worry, because this book is here to help you out! Take as much time as you need to improve yourself and you will soon find yourself impressed with your own progress.

If you scored between a 20 and 39:

Your honesty is something to be admired! While your confidence may not be at a scale that you would prefer, you must know that you have the power to elevate it. You can find all the help you need in this book. Much excitement awaits you because you are about to transform your life for the better.

Now that you know what your current level of confidence is, the next step is to take a look at any of the areas that you strongly agreed and disagreed with. These reveal much of who you are.

For instance, if you strongly disagreed with 13, then it probably means you often feel isolated from others. Perhaps you should spend more time with good friends who can give you a fresh perspective.

And let's say you strongly agreed with 11, then it means you are sensitive and aware towards other people's perception of you. This is a strength just as long as you pay more attention to the positive and constructive side of it.

Overall, these highlights can help you tailor-fit a program, which is most suitable for your needs.

Keep in mind that everyone can harness the qualities of a self-confident person. And while any of these qualities may ebb and flow throughout life, it always helps to stay grounded by knowing the type of person you want to become.

The Qualities of a Self-Confident Person

Have you ever tried something new and challenging, solved a problem, or demonstrated a skill? Did you go through with it even if you did not feel like it? Have you noticed that it wasn't actually that bad once you got to do it?

If you did, then your "it wasn't so bad" moment was actually a manifestation of confidence! It is getting out of your comfort zone to achieve something, and no matter how pressured it may have made you feel, you were able to do it.

When you are a self-confident person, you do not mind the feeling of discomfort that a new experience causes. That's because you believe in your ability to overcome it and achieve your goal. When you are confident, you inspire those around you to stop panicking and start taking action.

Now you may think that this is obviously easier said than done. How can you possibly not mind the discomfort when your heart starts to race and you break into a cold sweat?

Well, confident people started out that way, too. However, because they choose to believe in themselves, they learn to handle things with poise. Their breath is calm and steady rather than fast and short. Their mindset is all about being proactive and positive, instead of defensive and self-defeating.

To help you have a clearer picture of how to become more self-confident, here are the ten core qualities that will make you one:

A positive mindset

You know that there is always a good side in every story. You regard yourself in a positive light and you seek to see the good in others as well.

A sense of purpose

You have chosen or even carved your own path in life. You make all the different parts of who you are work together to achieve this purpose.

Good health

You respect and therefore care for your body and mind. You believe that your energy impacts your mood. This is why you make sure to nourish your body and give yourself time to rest and relax each day.

Emotional stability

You know that the best way to deal with a stressful situation is to stay calm and reasonable. You become aware when you start to feel strong emotions, specifically anxiety, sadness and anger, but you know how to respond to them well.

Motivation

You find ways to make your everyday tasks enjoyable, no matter how simple some may seem to be. You know how to focus and get into a "state of flow," or concentrate so well that nothing can distract you.

A desire to learn

You take pleasure in learning and experiencing something new. You see each day as an opportunity to develop yourself and you feel grateful for that. You never see yourself as an expert, but as a constant learner.

Chapter 3 The Power of Positive Thinking

Self-talk is literally the ability to talk to oneself. We engage in self-talk every day, from the thoughts we have inside our minds to the stories we tell ourselves.

All of life can be seen as a conversation, as stories. A story is essentially any belief, thought, or reality we tell ourselves is real. All of reality and the universe itself is an interweaving mix of stories, both individual and collective. In this respect, the mind is an incredibly powerful tool and can be seen as the root of everything. All problems, extraordinary creations, worries and concerns, genius ideas, fears and insecurities, and solutions stem from the mind. We, therefore, have the power to create, shape, and destroy through the power of our thoughts alone.

When we refer to creating, shaping, and destroying, there are some profound implications. The power to create is a gift, a blessing; the whole of life is an act of creation. Our minds being tools for doing so shows just how special we are. The ability to shape suggests we can literally restructure the world around us with our thoughts, beliefs, intentions, perceptions, and impressions. There is great power in self-talk reshaping and restructuring our environments. Finally, the power to destroy or destruct teaches us just how essential it is to engage in positive, healthy, and healing self-talk and thinking, not just for ourselves but for others.

What do we mean when we say healing? Well, it is rather simple! All of life involves duality: light and dark, day and night, creation and destruction. Everything can be seen to exist in a state of balance, equilibrium, and wholeness. The planet herself aims to retain wholeness as she is one living, conscious entity, all of the different parts interacting to make up the whole. Simultaneously our bodies are designed to achieve and maintain homeostasis, a state of balance, health, and equilibrium. In this respect, it can be suggested that the planet, our own bodies, and all of life itself are in a constant state of healing, forever seeking to achieve and maintain wholeness.

Our minds are the tools for doing so. The mind is a powerful thing, and daily life can either be heaven or hell based on the stories, the self-talk we tell ourselves. If our thoughts have such a powerful influence on not only our inner world but our outer worlds, this suggests that harnessing the force of self-talk and positive thinking could be one of the most important, beneficial, and self- loving things we do for ourselves. In the rest of the book, we will explore exactly how to do so.

How to Think Positively

Thinking positively is very similar to self-talk, although not identical. Just as self-talk is the conversations we have with ourselves, thinking positively, or positive thinking, is the energy, direction, and focus we give our conversations. Now, at this stage, it is important to note that thinking positively is not synergistic with being happy or joyful all the time. There are many cases in life where one needs or wants to think positively when their feelings, inner world, or some external situation may actually be very painful, sad, or neutral. Having a positive mindset, or engaging in positive thinking, is the ability to apply a positive and optimistic outlook to any situation in life with the intention of bettering oneself, another, or some situation or scenario. Applying positive thinking to self-talk, therefore, can have some wonderful effects.

Combining positive thinking with the stories we tell ourselves can improve all aspects of life. Relationships, both intimate and platonic, work, health and vitality, focus and concentration, abilities and mindset, passion and excitement for life, and the openness to learn and engage in personal projects, dreams, and ambitions are all areas that can be enhanced greatly with positive self-talk. As the self is a complex, interactive, holistic, and rather extraordinary thing, applying positive thinking and mental patterns is something that will benefit us greatly.

So how do we think positively? Well, as already shared, thinking positively is not all about rainbows and unicorns. Positive thinking is accepting and embracing the shadow, those dark or less favorable aspects of both self and life, and choosing to focus on one's positives. The key is being conscious.

A choice is a very important factor when reshaping and restructuring thoughts. When we choose to think positively, we are literally restructuring, recalibrating, and reshaping our brains, the neurons inside and the mental thought patterns and programs that affect daily life. Our thoughts, as you are aware, have a profound influence on everything, both our inner world and internal health and our outer environment. So, shifting perspectives to ones more in alignment and harmony with a reality rooted in love, positivity, unity, connection, abundance, bliss, new opportunities and experiences, and anything and everything else associated with a positive, healthy mindset actively influences the focus of our awareness.

The best analogy to use is to imagine a spotlight. Picture the universe, the sky and stars at night, and equate it with consciousness (the unconscious mind, subconscious mind, and conscious mind: all of consciousness and thought). Now visualize shining a torch into the night sky with a focused intention of lighting up one specific star, planet, or faraway galaxy. The light is your intention and focus.

You are still aware that all of the other stars, planets, and galaxies exist, but in that moment of shining your light directly on one object, thing, or place, your mind became attuned to it. Your awareness shifted, and everything else in the sky, all of the other elements of consciousness, of the universe, ceased to exist. They, of course, were still always there, but the point is that in those moments of directed awareness and intended focus, the only thing that had all your energy and mental concentration was the thing you chose to shine your light on. You were intentionally lighting up something.

This is essentially what happens when we choose consciously to engage in positive thinking. The darkness and all other elements of existence are still there and exist; it is just our focus that actively and consciously has a profound effect on whatever we are shining our light at or on. This can be seen to be the fundamental essence of thinking positively: that there will always be light and dark, shine and shadow, but we always have the choice to shine the light. Our minds have the power to illuminate.

Positive thinking can be achieved through many methods, including neurolinguistics programming, meditation and mindfulness, mantras and affirmations, cognitive shaping, certain forms of sound therapy such as binaural beats, and self-hypnosis/positive self-talk. Some of these we will explore in depth throughout the rest of these chapters.

Chapter 4 Advantages of Boosting Self-Confidence and Self-Esteem

Below are the five benefits that come with boosting self-esteem:

• Self-esteem increases your assertiveness

• Self-esteem increases your confidence in decision-making

• Self-esteem helps you feel safe, secure, and honest in relationships

• Self-esteem lowers the likelihood of staying in an unhealthy relationship

• Self-esteem helps you develop realistic expectations of yourself and others

• Self-esteem increases resilience to stress and obstacles

Self-Esteem Increases Your Assertiveness

Assertiveness is a skill that is absolutely necessary for a person to live a balanced life. When a person has self-esteem, it helps them a lot by creating a strong belief around the things they are saying, doing, and asking. If a person believes that want or need something, then they don't need to spend time thinking about whether or not people think it is true. People that have low self-esteem struggle with assertiveness because they have a fear of being judged or rejected. They think that asking for something is a sign of weakness, and therefore they will be judged for asking for something that they need. On the contrary, a person with a healthy self-esteem does not have fear about asking for what they need because no doubt has crossed their mind about it. Self-esteem comes from loving and respecting yourself, so for those that have this care for themselves will feel very normal, asking for the things they want and need.

To explain assertiveness a little further, I will provide you with a simple example. Imagine if your mother asked you to go over to her house as soon as possible to help her pack and move her things in preparation of her moving. However, you have had a rough week at work, so you already planned to spend your evening doing relaxing activities like watching a movie and taking a hot bath. Assertiveness, in this case, means being able to value your own needs just as much as you value other people's, like your mother's. A person with healthy self-esteem in this situation would say "I am worthy and deserve this break because I know I need it." A person with low self-esteem may say, "It would be selfish of me to have a relaxing night when somebody is asking for my help." An important part of self-esteem is understanding the fact that a person cannot pour from a glass that is empty. In this example, if the person had low self-esteem, they will probably go and help their mother move despite feeling very tired and will end up feeling like other people don't respect their time. However, people will not know how you feel until they communicate their feelings, so it is not the fault of the mother for simply asking for help.

Here is one more example of assertiveness. This time, the example will be in the workplace. Imagine if your boss had just asked you for the third time this month to step in and finish your co-worker's report because he has fallen behind on his schedule once again, and your boss knows that you are a more efficient employee compared to him. A person who has healthy self-esteem would say, "This is the third time you've asked me this month to take on extra work because John is behind schedule again. I value deeply being a team player, but I feel extra stressed and overwhelmed when I am constantly doing extra work. What can we do to make sure this doesn't happen again?" This is the ideal way to respond to your boss in this situation because you have to have enough self-respect to tell them that enough is enough and that you don't appreciate always being taken advantage of. A person with low self-esteem in this situation would likely just agree to take on the extra work but end up resenting their coworker for it. They will likely drain themselves too much due to the extra work and end up blaming others for it, thus fostering unhealthy relationships. By communicating with other people and letting them know your feelings will give them a chance to understand where you are coming from and adjust their own actions accordingly.

Learning to be assertive is a required life skill that is very important due to how frequently it is used and respected. If you think you are a person that is suffering from the "yes" syndrome, the first step you should take may be to start working on your self-esteem to help you recognize and respect your own wants and needs. Do keep in mind that being assertive is not the same as being aggressive. Assertiveness is all about being firm and clear about what they need/want, while aggression is about being demanding. The way a person delivers their message using a tone of voice and body language heavily influences the way people perceive your request.

Self-Esteem Increases Your Confidence in Decision Making

The second benefit that comes with having a healthy self-esteem is the ability to improve decision-making confidence. Due to the fact that a person's life is mainly determined by the decisions they make, people who don't have self-esteem are heavily affected by the anxiety of that truth. When a person has self-esteem, they are able to recognize their own wants and needs. By knowing what those things are, it makes the process of decision making a lot simpler since you already understand your goal/intention, and you are dedicated to making a decision that will lead to that goal. People with little to no self-esteem often spend a lot of time debating with themselves and playing out every scenario of failure in their minds. They get caught up in the nervousness of what other people might say or think about their decision.

Self-Esteem Helps You Feel Safe, Secure, and Honest in Relationships

Have you ever heard the famous saying 'you must learn to love yourself before you can love other people'? This saying holds true on the topic that we are about to talk about. One of the biggest benefits of having self-esteem is having the ability to love and respect yourself. Having this means that you won't be as likely to seek out respect and love from other people, which often leads to unhealthy relationships. You will feel more safe and secure during relationships due to the value you feel in yourself.

Self-Esteem Lowers the Likelihood of Staying in an Unhealthy Relationship

Self-esteem helps people feel safe, secure, and honest when they are in a relationship. It also helps people realize when the relationship is an unhealthy one. The theory behind this is very simple; if a person has healthy self-esteem, they are able to recognize their wants, needs, and opinions and will prioritize those things when making decisions. However, if a person has low self-esteem, they are unable to identify those things. Therefore, they will not be able to prioritize them. The dictionary definition of an unhealthy relationship is where at least one person in this relationship is showcasing unhealthy behaviors or that their behavior does not come from a place of respect for the other person.

Self-Esteem Helps You Develop Realistic Expectations of Yourself and Others

Throughout the course of a person's life, they likely have set unrealistic expectations for themselves. For instance, some people strive to be an Olympian by the age of 18 without any prior athletic experience, or they may be wanting to become the CEO of a million-dollar business by the age of 22. The main difference between unrealistic expectations set by people with low self-esteem compared to people with healthy self-esteem is that the person with low self-esteem will judge themselves harshly when they cannot achieve their unrealistic expectations.

Self-Esteem Increases Resilience to Stress and Obstacles

Scientific studies have shown the link between healthy self-esteem and a person experiencing less stress overall. Since self-esteem impacts a person's happiness directly, it also contributes heavily to a person's feelings about their life. If a person is able to trust in their own ability to overcome an obstacle, then they can see difficult situations as challenges and not as threats. However, if a person isn't able to trust in their own ability to handle stressful situations, they will likely see them as threatening. Self-efficacy is the dictionary term that describes a person's ability to feel capable and resourceful. Self-efficacy is another important component that plays a role in self-esteem and stress management.

Benefits of Boosting Self-Confidence

Very similar to self-esteem, there are numerous benefits that can be gained when a person increases their self-confidence. At this point in the book, we have learned that when self-esteem is increased, it also increases a person's self-confidence as well. Since the effects of self-confidence are more external, its benefits tend to be more on the external side as well. People are often capable of hiding their low self-esteem, but self-confidence is a lot more difficult to hide. In order to discover that somebody has low self-esteem comes from getting to know them through deep conversations and spending a lot of time around them. However, discovering that a person has low self-confidence can be as simple as just watching their physical posture, comfortability, and social ability. By increasing self-confidence, a person can change the outcomes of their actions and gain respect from other people. Self-confidence is an important trait for the people that work in a team environment. People with more self-confidence are able to encourage a more collaborative working environment where people are able to express their opinions and ideas rather than just going along with what other people suggest. The ability to share thoughts and opinions diplomatically is a skill that is highly sought after in leadership roles. Here are the benefits that come with having higher self-confidence:

• Increasing self-confidence increases overall performance

• Increasing self-confidence increases overall happiness

• Increasing self-confidence increases social abilities

• Improving self-confidence improves physical and mental health

Increasing Self-Confidence Increases Overall Happiness

When a person's self-confidence increases, it is related directly to bettering their overall performance. For instance, when a person is starting something new like a video game or a new sport, they will naturally get better as they practice. When a person is starting something new, it is normal that they may have lower confidence on the first day. However, when they start to get better at it, they will develop more confidence naturally when they know that their skills have improved. This example shows exactly how self-confidence can affect a person's overall performance in any task in life. People who start new things having higher confidence levels tend to be better at those tasks right at the beginning compared to the people who have lower self-confidence.

Increasing Self-Confidence Increases Overall Happiness

When a person has a good amount of self-confidence, they naturally feel more confident when they are doing tasks, which ultimately leads to a higher success rate; therefore, they are able to feel good about themselves, which leads to more confidence and then to more happiness. Professionals who work in Confidence Building programs and workshops Often report that people who have more life satisfaction and are happier tend to show more self-confidence.

Increasing Self-Confidence Increases Social Ability

People that have good self-confidence levels tend to be more relaxed in social situations or during an initial meeting interaction. When self-confidence is there, a person's belief in themselves is an internal component and is not affected by other people's judgments. People like this have the ability to move stress-free during social interactions without fearing rejection. Psychologists have said that self-confidence creates a feeling of comfort when people are faced with a challenge. Those that are confident feel excited regarding their future and are more comfortable when expressing it to others. Since they are more confident and excited, they also carry themselves in that way and are able to have conversations with more excitement and ease. Due to this, confident people feel more at ease in a lot of social situations, and this trait draws a lot of attention from other people. They tend to emit a positive energy that is very desirable and contagious to others.

Improving Self-Confidence Improve Physical and Mental Health

According to the professionals at the National Mental Health Centre, healthy self-esteem and self-confidence are the prime indicators of good mental wellbeing. As we already learned earlier in this book, a person's self-esteem is often developed in their early stages of childhood, where their parents were responsible for building their confidence level and character. Children that grew up in families that were more positive and encouraging tend to have more confidence later on in life, which allows them to do better in school, sports, social skills, and just take better care of themselves in general. When children grow up into their teens, the ones with healthy self-confidence are able to handle peer pressure better and can make decisions based on their best interests.

Using the theory of the mind and body connection, it says that a person's physical health is affected by their mental health and the other way around as well. People who suffer from mental disorders like depression and anxiety often have weakened physical health, such as chronic pain or a lower immunity to diseases. A person that is taking care of themselves physically, like exercising and eating healthy, can help them improve their physical health, but having good mental wellbeing can also help a person prevent physical problems.

People who have good physical health tend to have more happiness and satisfaction in life because they are able to do more things in general. They typically have more energy and motivation to get themselves out into the world to accomplish things or simply just to connect with other people. Humans naturally feed off of other human's happiness, so when people are spending time with others that are confident and happy, they can also begin to feel that way too. This is the reason why you often see people that are confident hanging out in the same social circles. People that have good mental health are attracted to those that are the same and would prefer to spend their time around those people rather than others who don't exhibit the same traits.

Chapter 5 Setting Your Goals

Personal Vision

This is your vital aspect for making a strong, feasible life plan. Contribute time to consider all that you put stock in and all that you might want your life to be about. Concentrate on what impact you need your life to have on your family, your companions, and everybody you meet.

Note your thoughts in a diary or utilize your PC. Run down anything that has significance to you. Take as much time as is needed and get it perfectly clear.

Your Strengths

Write down the majority of Your Strengths. From that point onward, list any feeble zones.

Presently this is basic - annihilate the rundown of shortcomings and spotlight absolutely on Your Strengths.

After you have Your Personal Vision and Your Strengths obviously characterized it turns out to be anything but difficult to...

Characterize Your Goals and Desired Outcomes

Audit Personal Vision and Your Strengths a couple of times and after that challenge to dream a tad. Concentrate on what you need your life to resemble in the event that you have a boundless stockpile of cash, assets, and time.

Run down anything you might want to have, do, and accomplish. Record the spots you'd like to visit, individuals you might want to meet, things you might want to learn, and encounters you might want to have.

Next, choose one want that you want to achieve rapidly and effectively. Work it out in detail. This will assist you with valuing the intensity of this basic framework.

Your Why

When you recognize what you want to accomplish, characterize Your Why. Consider what it will intend to you when you achieve this unequivocal result. Imagine yourself having finished it. Presently, directly beneath your goal, record whatever achieving this particular goal would intend to you. This is your self-inspirational power for making a move.

Your Massive Plan of Action

Alright, you have what you might want plainly characterized and you know why you want it. Presently ask yourself, "What are the moves that I should make so as to accomplish my result?" Write them out.

Goal setting and planning, encourages you see obviously what you have to do. The way to getting results is making a move.

Concentrate on what you have recorded and pick what you can do right away. Making predictable move is the key fixing that gets results. At the point when you get moving energy becomes an integral factor. You will achieve your particular result and make the most of Your Why.

Put this uncomplicated goal setting and planning framework vigorously for each result you have recorded. Put aside a period consistently to utilize this procedure and make a move each day.

Over the long haul, you will be astounded at how a lot of your life is winding up better.

The Importance of Goal and planning

In the event that you need to arrive at any degree of accomplishment in your life, it is important that you define goals and make arrangements. At the point when you set the goal and make the arrangement to accomplish a specific thing, that gives you a reasonable vision. A reasonable vision implies you know precisely what it is you need to achieve.

Mentors don't simply send their players out on the play field without first setting up an arrangement. So, can any anyone explain why we experience life now and then and not have an unmistakable vision with respect to what we ask for from it?

Defining the goal and making the arrangement plants a dream in your psyche and furthermore your subliminal personality.

During this procedure, the subliminal personality is given a lot of guidelines to pursue and complete. It's normal if your arrangement changes every now and then inasmuch as you keep your mind concentrated on the goal. By doing so the arrangement will at last succeed.

To prevail in life, you should set your goals, get an arrangement, tail it and remain centered. It is critical to stay centered or you'll lose locate. When you dismiss the goal, you will disregard the arrangement and in a little while everything will self-destruct. Why would that be? Since when you quit concentrating on the goal, you are telling your inner mind that the goal is never again significant. Thus, the subliminal personality quits chipping away at making your specific goal a reality.

Staying center isn't a simple undertaking. Your psyche resembles its very own individual, as though it is totally isolated from you. Despite the fact that you might need to do, be and accomplish a specific thing, your mind will need to keep accomplishing things the manner in which it is used to. It will be obstinate and set up an extraordinary battle. Your mind will give all of you sorts of opposition, even guide you to abandon your fantasies.

So how would you get your brain to tune in and consent to changes? By being constant and remaining submitted by continually thinking about your goals. Search for chances to grasp and invite change. Ensure that you set practical goals.

Start little and recognize and commend your little triumphs continually.

At last, your mind will start to comprehend and acknowledge the progressions, and before you know it, your psyche is working with the procedure and the cycle of your goals turning into a reality has begun. Defining goals, getting an arrangement and remaining centered rises to progress.

It is not uncommon for people to be naturally geared toward success. While some people are content living the life they have, people generally want to keep advancing. They want to drive a better car, move into a nicer house, have a better physique, be healthier, and excel in their career. Even though people naturally want to climb up the ladder in their life, however, it does not necessarily mean this is a reality. One of the things that set those who want and those who succeed apart is the ability to set goals.

You cannot expect to get anywhere in life unless you set goals. With a goal, you gain the ability to hold yourself accountable for whatever you are striving toward. Let's look at the example of someone trying to lose weight—if they set a goal that they want to lose ten pounds by the end of the month, but they continue to eat unhealthy foods and lead an inactive lifestyle, they are not going to meet their goal. Then, when the end of the month comes around, they can hold themselves accountable for not losing that weight. While they may experience a little disappointment, failing their goal gives them time to re-evaluate what they want. It is the opportunity to try again, but to try harder this time.

Benefits of Goal-Setting

Goal setting does more than increasing a person's chance of success. Here's a look at why you should set goals:

● Faster movement toward your goal- Do you ever feel as if you are sleepwalking through life? This feeling is common for many people, as they work hard and still do not achieve what they want. Students finish college with a degree, but still do not know what they want to do as a career. Adults settle into jobs outside of their dream career, mostly because settling is easier. The reason they do not succeed is that their hard work is directionless. When you set goals, you have a clear idea of what you want. This helps you decide if an action is going to bring you closer to or farther from your goal. It helps you align your choices and make everything you do a reflection of your effort to achieve your goals. The reality is that when you are not working toward your other goals, you are working toward someone else's. Someone who gives in and cheats on their diet is working toward meeting the fast food industry's goals—lining their pockets. A person who is stuck in a dead-end job is meeting their boss' goals—to have loyal employees that work hard, even though they don't necessarily strive for more. When you start setting goals, you free yourself from the trap of living on autopilot and you gain the ability to reach goals faster. It helps you become conscious of what you are creating in your life so you can proactively work toward those things you want to become a reality for yourself.

• Knowledge of when you veer off track- Even people who are set in their goals slip up. They may mis-evaluate something or have a setback that moves them farther away from their plan. However, re-evaluation is a key element of goal-setting. You should not only set goals for this week and this month, but you should also set goals for one year from now, three years from now, and even five years from now. Once you are thinking this far ahead, it becomes easier to create smaller goals that are more achievable. Once you have an actionable plan, you can set things in motion and work toward your goal. Everything in life is created twice—once in the mind and then again in the real world. If you don't use goal-setting to mentally create your goals, you cannot physically create them either.

• Increased accountability- Even the people closest to you may cloud your goals with their own. Someone who has decided to spend their nights studying to further their career may be convinced to go out with their friend instead. This friend is more interested in their own goal of having fun, rather than supporting their friend in their educational endeavor.

• Greater motivation- The best goals are those that are set from a place of passion. Your goals should lead you toward the best life that you want to live. For you to want this life, you must choose goals that align with your core values and those things you want to make a reality for yourself. By setting long-term goals and re-evaluating them, you always have something greater to strive for.

• Ability to reach your highest potential- Many people do not live up to their full potential. They have unique skills and talents that go untapped. This is especially true for people who settle in life. When you assume that you have become all you are going to be, there is not necessarily a point to learn new things or focus on progress. By setting goals for what you want to achieve, you work to improve your skills and talents.

• Better ability to overcome obstacles- When you have forward motion, the bumps that you hit in the road become things you trip over on your way to your goal. Rather than staying stuck when something doesn't go your way, you know that you need to get up and keep moving toward your goal. This can help you overcome some of the most challenging times in your life.

Setting Goals to Grow Your Confidence and Self-Esteem

As you develop greater confidence and self-esteem, you are going to enhance your ability to strive for your goals. People who are confident in themselves aren't afraid to do something that is difficult or challenging in pursuit of a goal. They are confident enough to step outside of their comfort zone, as well as confident enough to know if they do fail, they will survive it and be better people because of it. Having high self-esteem also helps in the creation and achievement of goals. When you love yourself enough to embrace change and work toward improving your life, it makes a major difference in your life.

For a goal to be an effective motivator, it is generally agreed upon that goals should be SMART, meaning:

Specific- Creating a specific goal means adding details that help keep you motivated on track. It is easy for someone to say they want to lose weight and still feel upset when a month passes and they only lose one or two pounds. This would be okay if they were only trying to lose one or two pounds by the end of the month. Since their goal was vague, however, they feel disappointed even though they have technically lost weight. Setting a specific goal is also important for creating a sense of motivation and accountability.

Measurable- Goals should be measurable in some way. This can be tricky when you are trying to measure something like self-esteem or confidence since you cannot assign a number to it. A better way to measure something like confidence or self-esteem is to set specific goals. For example, you might increase your self-confidence at work by making it your goal to speak up during the morning meeting one time. From there, you might volunteer to work with someone else on a project. To measure self-esteem, you might make it your goal to challenge negative thoughts for a full day instead of letting them rattle around in your brain. Even though you cannot assign a number, you still know that you are achieving a goal that brings you closer to growing your self-esteem and self-confidence.

Achievable- For someone lacking in confidence, one of the most detrimental things they can do is set a goal that is difficult or impossible to achieve. Imagine that someone sets the goal of losing fifty pounds within a month. To reach this, they would have to lose more than a pound a day. That would require an amount of calorie restriction and exercise that could be detrimental to their health. Additionally, when they set a goal this ambitious and fail, it discourages them from continuing on their path to achieving that weight loss. They might experience a setback or return to their old habits because they feel discouraged.

Relevant- When a goal is relevant, it means that it is reasonable and aligned with your values and passions. You will have trouble motivating yourself to do something that you do not want enough. For example, someone who puts in the work to be a doctor may find themselves struggling to apply for research grants or do work to further the field of medicine because they do not feel passionate about it. They may even struggle through medical school and their residency, as these are things that take a great deal of work and focus. It is much better to set goals for yourself that relate to your passion and where you want to go in life. Otherwise, you are wasting time doing something that you do not love—when you could be spending time reaching goals that will make you happy.

Time-bound- A goal that is time-bound is one that has a specific restriction on when you want to complete it. By setting a deadline for yourself, you are increasing the pressure and boosting motivation. Without a deadline, you may move leisurely toward your goal. This means you achieve it at a much slower rate than you would expect to.

Chapter 6 Exercises to Gain Self-Confidence

Lack of self-confidence is an evil faced by a multitude of people in their personal and professional development. Indeed, it is not given to everyone to look fulfilled, smiling, and comfortable in all circumstances! If the causes of lack of self-confidence are varied and specific to each, there are fortunately some simple solutions. Operating in general, they allow making a good impression and achieve its objectives.

A person who lacks self-confidence will often be anxious, nervous, and will act unnaturally in his relationships with others. The fear of being judged negatively will cause her to withdraw into herself and no longer dare to open outward. The origin of this discomfort sometimes seems very minimal compared to its consequences. A small remark slipped by your piano teacher, and you are convinced you do not have the musical ear, a criticism during a presentation that goes back to elementary school, and you can no longer speak in public... A lack of self-confidence often manifests itself in situations where, on the contrary, you should seem comfortable to inspire trust. For example, during a job interview, a date, or even to ask for advice in everyday life.

To protect yourself, you hide behind a character, often caricatured, who does not necessarily correspond to you. This increases your discomfort compared to others. Also, you lose a bright look at yourself, and you no longer know what suits you. By being less and less daring, you move away from your opportunities, and you have the impression of being constantly confronted with failure. You think it is useless to try a competition because you do not have the necessary level, or that it is not worth sending your CV, because your profile is not interesting., you have to dare at least once to prove to yourself that you can bring positive things to others.

But how do you gain confidence?

As the Americans say, "fake it until you make it," which can be translated into "pretend until you do it." Achieving a sense of self-confidence will create a positive image of yourself and help make you more confident. To do this, there are some straightforward actions to accomplish. Taking care of your physical appearance is one. You feel more confident when you feel clean, well dressed, and well-shaved to talk to someone. Wearing close-fitting, colorful clothes, washing you every day, taking a quick look in the mirror. These are all simple actions that can be carried out every day. Your attitude is also essential: you must not hesitate to look up with sincerity, to smile, to stand straight, to express yourself clearly.

It is also essential to know yourself well to be able to show self-confidence. Know not only its origins and tastes but also its character and its strong and weak points. These are things that you will be asked in a job interview, but that will also allow you to make your own choices without being influenced by others. And making a choice that suits you, that suits your way of working and your tastes, is already guaranteeing part of your success. No need to try to be a mountain guide if you can't stand the altitude, or to be a fildefériste if you feel dizzy! Everyone has personal skills, even if it's not so easy to identify and know how to use them. You must, therefore, be attentive to your habits: realize that you are helpful, able to organize a successful evening or simmer small dishes, that you like complex calculations or manual work. Know what we love and what we can do allows us to position ourselves in front of the world, and to be sure of ourselves.

Self-confidence is a feeling that is far from being innate; it is acquired. However, faced with the multiple problems linked to a lack of self-esteem - often difficult to overcome - it is important to do personal work to gain confidence and thus achieve fulfillment. Between being complexed by your body, losing your means when it comes to speaking in public, and the inability to reach out to others, lack of self-esteem comes in different forms. From one individual to another. Insofar as self-confidence is not earned, but it is collected, everyone must, therefore, give of themselves to find confidence. As part of this personal work that awaits you, here are a dozen simple but effective exercises to practice to gain self-esteem, mental training approved by personal development experts.

Systematically take stock

The first thing he does remember about self-confidence or lack of confidence is that it is a feeling specific to an area of your life. You can, for example, be very comfortable in love life and not at all professionally. Also, the first Self-Confidence Exercise that you absolutely must practice is the inventory. Concretely, you must define the main areas of your life, such as work, love, health, friendships. to proceed with an honest rating. This exercise allows you to realize in which specific areas you feel most uncomfortable, in which you are benevolent and in which you usually act.

On the one hand, the objective of this exercise is to learn how to regain self-confidence in the areas that are most important to you. On the other hand, this training helps you to become aware of your feelings of unease, such as tremors, anxiety, inability to speak, or hesitation. Identifying the triggers for your lack of confidence allows you to look for the root cause of your discomfort, and get behind it to find the solution to your pain. If it is in the professional context that you feel your lack of confidence the most, try to understand what is causing your pain, working environment, unpleasant colleagues. Then ask yourself what you can do to change things and not endure them permanently.

Favor self-criticism over comparison

When it comes to gaining confidence, the most recommended exercise or even self-confidence record is self-criticism. If some people find it so hard to overcome their lack of confidence, it is often due to the comparison they make of themselves by their contribution to others. To make a difference, use your judgment to restore your image and gain self-esteem. The work you have to do here starts with training yourself to be treated with kindness, an exercise that is sometimes difficult, but essential. Rather than telling you that you have had romantic failures, put things in perspective, and tell yourself that you have been rejected like everyone else.

Self-criticism is the first step towards self-confidence, as it allows you to dissociate the negative image you have of yourself and reality. Indeed, the truth is such that, like everyone else, you have your weaknesses and your strengths, a token of your authenticity in the eyes of the rest of the world. Stop focusing on your negative side, and learn to discover the best of your personality. You must also stop looking for perfection at all costs because nobody is just perfect. Why would you be? Dare to be self-critical is to get to know yourself better and ultimately accept yourself as you are.

Become aware of its qualities

To achieve acceptance, the best thing to do is to realize its qualities. To effectively carry out this exercise, remember to put on paper the list of your classes, namely organized, intelligent, faithful, daring, calm, courageous, and resourceful. Make sure you are as honest as possible and do not hesitate to gradually add the qualities that you discover. Also know that when your entourage compliments you, for example lovable, beautiful, and funny, etc., it is undoubtedly true. These compliments will then complete your list of qualities. At the same time, make a diagnosis of your faults representing your weaknesses, which you will also make a written list of.

Therein lies the difficulty of this exercise; it is to launch yourself into small daily challenges to improve your qualities on the one hand. On the other hand, learn to face your weaknesses, which is essential for successfully fighting these blockages quite merely. At the end of this exercise, you allow yourself to durably increase your confidence by improving yourself in the areas that you like and where you are gifted, such as deepening gardening because of your quality of having a green thumb. You also realize that by facing your faults, you will practically make new strengths, new unsuspected qualities. Your shyness has always been a burden on you, so learn to open up to others, and without realizing it, you will have no trouble approaching a pure stranger.

Learn to appreciate yourself physically

Since what makes you unique is your personality and your physique, practicing real appreciation is particularly useful in gaining self-confidence. Realize that since you have to live with your body, you might as well make it an asset. Tall, short, thin or overweight, stick a photo of yourself - on which you have the most advantage - on the bathroom mirror or the fridge. To help you choose the picture, don't hesitate to ask your relatives or friends to define which photo highlights you the most.

The mere fact of seeing this photo daily helps you to stop losing your real worth at first. On the other hand, it is always difficult to appreciate yourself physically overnight. What you need to do in this case is to target what you like least about your home and work to improve it to make you stand out more. Admittedly, it is completely unimaginable to think of passing from 1,60 m to 1,75m. However, you can still give the impression of lengthening your legs by favoring high heels and highlight your femininity. Sometimes it takes just a little ingenuity to turn your imperfections into strengths.

Clarify your desires and needs

If eventually, you like your body even with your imperfections, you can always gain confidence by working on your needs and wishes. Personal development experts reveal that one of the leading causes of lack of self-confidence comes from the inability of the individual to clarify his wants and needs. Rather than always listening to this little voice telling you that you will never get there, take a step back and analyze in detail what your expectations are in life: building a family, a career in catering, offering you the journey of your dreams, give more time to one of your passions, etc.

The objective of this exercise is to understand precisely what you lack today to develop yourself personally, what blocks you and does not allow you to assert yourself in the end. Without realizing it, you spend your time thinking and imagining what you don't want, what scares you. Now, having confidence in yourself is precisely knowing what you want and giving yourself the means to get it. To better understand training, sit in front of the TV and watch a program that doesn't interest you. Rather than thinking of a show you want to watch, take the remote control and flip. Once you know what you want, take the initiative, take action, and make a difference.

Reconnect with the positive

As you can see, you are the only person who can change the life you are leading now. Be the change you are looking for. To achieve this, you absolutely must reconnect with the positive. The lack of self-confidence is often generated by an overly dominant-negative view, such as "I was not selected for this position because I do not have the necessary skills; I'm still single because I have no charm. " Rather than moping about your fate, practice daily to reconnect with the positive by taking stock of all the positive things that have happened during your days.

Reconnecting with the positive allows you to accept reality, but above all, to learn to rejoice in what is right. In other words, it is enough to learn to appreciate the right sides of things rather than focusing on negative thoughts. As part of this exercise, you can also dive back into one or more bright memories, which make you feel better and see things differently. The goal of this training is to change your outlook on life in general and to make better decisions. You have made mistakes in the past, which is by no means inevitable. Tell yourself that it saves you from reproducing them in the future and only learning from them.

List your achievements

To adopt a positive attitude daily, you can also exercise yourself by making a daily list of your accomplishments. Stop thinking about your failures and take stock of everything you have accomplished. From the most important to the one that seems minimal, write down on paper all of your accomplishments for the day, such as carrying out an essential task on time, speaking in public without hesitation. The more your daily achievements, the more confidence will be born in you. Itself. You will realize what an active and successful person you are, which increases your self-esteem.

By making a daily list of your accomplishments, you will unconsciously be born with the urge to always do better. You've been able to cut your cigarette consumption by one rod, so tomorrow make sure you smoke two fewer cigarettes and so on. In this way, you will gain motivation in your smoking cessation process, and boost your self-confidence regarding the achievement of your goal: to quit smoking. In this example, you will realize that each of your small victories leads you to the success of your project, whatever its nature.

Assert yourself in all circumstances

Also, if the self-confidence exercises seem accessible to everyone at first, some present a more severe difficulty. This is also the case for the next training session, which consists of asserting oneself in all circumstances. As difficult as it may seem, this exercise is necessary so as not to be influenced by fear. The goal here is to be able to keep your ideas and argue them as well. Being assertive means knowing how to showcase yourself as you are, without fear of being judged by anyone, or to please others.

There are different alternatives for practicing this exercise. You can, for example, train by participating regularly in debates, the ideal opportunity to learn to defend your ideas, so to assert yourself. You can also submit yourself by working on your style of clothing, favoring the clothes that highlight you and in which you feel comfortable. Why do you insist on wearing a skirt if the pants are more convenient for you? Also think about buying clothes that you like, which are your size, even if it doesn't seem like a fashion victim, but rather like a person with his style and good about himself.

Take risks to better manage your emotions

Regaining self-confidence also means being able to take risks. Often, a lack of confidence creates fear of the unknown in you, preventing you from taking the lead. But taking risks is learning to live and discover new things. Insofar as you get stuck on your doubts, without realizing it, you feed on all kinds of negative emotions, fear, stress. Yet by taking risks, you learn to manage your emotions better, and by at the same time, you build up positive feelings generated by your discoveries and all these new experiences available to you.

To take risks is to face your fears. Your job no longer satisfies you at different levels - salary, hours, lack of recognition from your employer, or others - so take the risk of looking for a job that suits you best. Taking risks is effectively leaving your comfort zone to aspire to a better life, and therefore to feel happier. The idea of risk-taking is indeed based on your quest for well-being, whether professionally or in the context of sentimental life. Put your doubts aside and act to make a real difference in your life. You may experience setbacks, but you will feel satisfied when you realize that you still managed to try your luck despite your apprehensions.

Create contact

Finally, the best exercise in self-confidence remains the creation of contact. It is clear that when a person lacks confidence, his most significant handicap is not being able to open up to others. However, it is precisely the fact of remaining closed in on oneself, which does not allow one to regain self-confidence. In this approach, create contact by addressing yourself to a work colleague, for example, by starting with greetings of use, then why not by asking it for professional advice. Also, repeat this exercise with people you want to do not know particularly, as your neighbor, to compensate, among others.

One of the worst things for your self-confidence is to stay focused on your problems. It's impossible to ignore all of your questions, but more efficient time management will focus on solutions. It will not be limited to increasing the level of your self-confidence

Chapter 7 Comfort Zones

The term "comfort zone" just sounds nice, doesn't it? It brings to mind a sanctuary where we're safe, taken care of and, well, comfortable. However, that imagery is deceiving. It tricks us into thinking that comfort zones are where we are supposed to be when, in reality; they're slowly draining the life from us.

To cultivate mental toughness, it's necessary to know what comfort zones are, how they work, and why we should ditch them as fast as we can.

What Is a Comfort Zone?

The general definition of a comfort zone is a psychological state in which your environment and routines promote feelings of safety and are devoid of anxiety or stress. An important thing to note, however, is that this doesn't translate to happiness necessarily. For a while, we may be content in comfort zones. After all, that's what they're there for. We may be with a partner we are reluctant to leave because we've become used to being with them, working a job that doesn't satisfy us but is "good enough," and living in a city that's strangling our potential but moving would be too big a change.

Comfort zones are those boxes or boundaries we put ourselves in that mental toughness helps us push past or climb over. You'll find out how soon.

Why We Have Comfort Zones

Simple: we crave safety. Back when we were living in the bush and half the animal kingdom wanted to eat us, comfort zones were physical places where we could let our guard down and relax for a short while. These may have been caves, camps, or small villages. Comfort zones were essentially safety zones, and in those days, that was just fine.

Enter the modern age. Comfort zones are no longer physical but psychological. We have taken the places that offered safety and put them in our minds, associating the lack of stress or anxiety with something positive. However, since the element of life or death is gone, comfort zones now act as limitations rather than an evolutionary advantage.

When something is new, different, or uncertain, it scares us. Our brains tell us that change is bad, and since our brains are usually right, we listen without question. Even if we feel a deep craving for something more, we stick to what we know to avoid pain. Comfort zones are survival mechanisms, but they're outdated.

How Your Comfort Zone Is Holding You Back

Here's the real problem with comfort zones: they put up barriers that separate you from your potential. It's like being in a city where all the propaganda is telling you is that life's great, but you can see through the chain-link fence to the other side and want to know what's out there. It takes courage to climb over or tunnel under that fence, and the longer you stay in your comfort zone, the less likely you are to try to escape.

Comfort zones stop us from realizing our potential and living our lives. We often settle in them because we feel like we have to be grateful for where we're at and that asking for more would be greedy. If you have a home, someone who loves you, and a good job, why upset the apple cart?

Because you'll never get where you want to be if you settle for "good enough."

Do you think Olympic athletes aim for second or third because they're almost first, and therefore close enough? Of course not. They aim to win. Every. Time. They reject comfort zones fully and completely. That's how they reach the top of their game.

It's time to do the same in your life. If you're still not convinced that comfort zones are actually killing your potential, consider some of these consequences that arise when you stick with what's safe and familiar:

•	You don't get to find out your true strength because you never push your limits.

•	Because you're always operating within the minimum requirements, you only see minimal results.

•   You don't learn and grow. In 10 years, you'll be exactly where you are now because you won't gain the experience needed to progress.

•   You forget what it means to truly live because you're stuck in the same routines that no longer serve you.

•   You'll be afraid to do what you really want to do and thus ignore your inner calling.

•   Once you realize your comfort zone is no longer comfortable, even the false sense of contentment will disappear. Unhappiness follows shortly after.

•   You'll never reach your goals. They exist outside your comfort zone.

In the end, it's far more ungrateful to live a small life than to embrace every opportunity this vast world has to offer.

How Do You Know If You're Stuck in a Comfort Zone?

Sometimes, we don't even realize we're in a comfort zone until something happens that wakes us up, or we smack into the barrier that we didn't know was there. Comfort zones are sneaky; they can pop up when we're not paying attention and only make themselves known when a new opportunity on the other side of the fence comes along and we're too uncertain to take it. If you're not sure if you're trapped in your comfort zone, read over a few of the signs to help you decide.

You Feel Like You're Stuck in a Rut

This is basically just another way of saying you're in your comfort zone, but it's a phrase we're more familiar with and it stirs up a sense of discontent that actually makes it easier for you to break free. While "comfort zone" sounds positive, "stuck in a rut" does not. It makes us think that we're not going anywhere—because we're not.

You might feel like you've had the same routine for too long or that you're not making any progress. Maybe life has become predictable and dull. When you have this feeling, don't despair. It's a good thing because it shows a desire for change. Use that to push yourself forward out of the rut.

You Avoid Anything New or Different

It's natural to be uncomfortable in a new situation or when you're doing something out of the ordinary, but if even the idea of change, of something outside your routine, makes you panic, that's a bad sign. When you're unwilling to expand your horizons or stray away from what's familiar out of fear, you're hiding behind the supposed safety provided by your comfort zone. You convince yourself that you're avoiding danger, but in reality you're avoiding discomfort. Nonetheless, a little discomfort is good. It shows that you have room to grow.

Mentally tough people seek out new experiences because they're instructive. They know they won't grow or learn if they don't try something out of the ordinary and step away from what's familiar. This doesn't mean they're not afraid. It means they don't let the fear control them.

You Don't Remember the Last Time You Asked for or Received a Raise

It might seem unrelated, but one aspect of mental toughness is asking for what you deserve. If you're not doing that, something's wrong.

If you haven't received a raise in a while, it could be because your job performance hasn't increased (which indicates you're in your comfort zone of ease and are "coasting"), or possibly because you are afraid to ask and get a "no." There's nothing wrong with knowing your value and demanding it be met with the appropriate compensation. When you respect yourself and your talents, you won't accept any less from others.

If, on the other hand, your job performance is to blame, look at why that is. Are you bored with your job and don't want to put effort in because you're not inspired? Do you feel unappreciated and thus have less of a reason to work hard? Both of these problems can be solved only if you step outside your comfort zone. Ask for what you deserve, and don't be content with anything less.

You're Not Working Towards Any Goals

Your life should always have a purpose and direction. Otherwise, you're just drifting. If you don't have any goals, or you've let your goals fall by the wayside, you'll naturally settle into a comfort zone. When we don't have goals or direction, we tend to stay put or drift. This lack of forward momentum helps erect comfort zone barriers. If you've been in the same place long enough, you'll begin to want to stay there because moving is too difficult.

Goals provide avenues for progress and act as guides that lead you to the next level of your life. Without them, you won't know which way to go, and you'll end up not going anywhere.

You've Lived in the Same and City and Been with the Same Person for Years, But You Don't Know Why

This book isn't out to give you dating advice or tell you to leave your loving partner. However, there's a difference between being in a relationship because you want to and being in one because you don't want to not be in a relationship and/or it's familiar. The people we spend the most time with have the biggest impact in our lives. If you're not happy with your partner, you won't be happy with yourself.

The same idea goes for your job. If you love your job, you feel fulfilled, and there's opportunity for growth. Then, of course, you'll want to stay for years. If you haven't advanced and don't enjoy what you do anymore, but you're too afraid to switch careers or companies, then you've made a nice, cushy comfort zone around yourself that guarantees financial security but sacrifices well-being.

Mental toughness requires evaluation. It can sometimes seem harsh, but it's necessary. You need to ask yourself the right questions and be honest about the answer. Comfort zones often bring with them a touch of denial, but you're not doing yourself any favors by pretending you're okay with the way things are. Ask yourself the following questions:

- Is this job helping me further my career?

- Am I in a city with plenty of opportunities for me?

- Does this job fit my passion?

- Do I feel like my life is meaningful?

- Does this situation serve me and my goals?

- Have I outgrown this person/job/city?

If you answer 'no' or "I don't know," you have some thinking to do. You should always feel like you're in the right place, not the easy one.

You Feel Like You Were Meant for More

...but you're afraid to ask what that "more" is. Although almost all of us have felt this at some point, how many of us listen to that call from within? We can still hear it when we're in our comfort zones, but we try to ignore it and bury it deeper. We feel like it's asking too much, especially if we already have lives that look successful. You can have a great job, beautiful house, fancy car, and thousands in the bank and still live within a comfort zone.

You're allowed to ask for more from life. That's what your entire existence is for! Not settling, not striving for "good enough," not giving up, and accepting that content must mean happy, even if it doesn't feel like it.

Mental toughness gives you the push needed to follow the call that tells you there's more out there for you. If you feel like you were meant for greater things, you are.

Strategies for Getting Out of Your Comfort Zone

It can be disheartening to realize that you've constructed walls around your life that stop you from pursuing what you truly want. That's not the end of the story, though. Now that you know you're in one, you can learn how to break out of your comfort zone. You don't have to leave it behind entirely or all at once, but start to test your limits and see how far you can push yourself. It won't be easy, of course. You'll need to learn how to deal with the stress that comes from taking chances and leverage resilience and discipline to keep you going when you want to quit.

For now, consider some of the following strategies to start pushing past the limitations you've set for yourself and break free.

Do What Scares You

This is perhaps the easiest and hardest way to escape your comfort zone. Anything that scares you is 100% outside your comfort zone because nothing in it stirs up feelings of fear, hence the comfort part.

So, what scares you? Are you afraid of asking for a raise? What about moving to a new city or even just a new neighborhood? Are you too nervous to ask out the person you've been eyeing at the coffee shop? Remember that mental toughness naturally involves a little fear, but overcoming that fear is what makes you tougher.

Start small and pick something that won't have massive repercussions. For instance, you're afraid to speak up in a meeting because you don't think your ideas will be accepted or appreciated. Do it anyway. What's the worst that can happen? No one listens. What's the best that may happen? Your boss finally sees that underneath that fear is a brilliant mind that's ready to handle bigger and better opportunities. Just like that, you're on a new trajectory because you have looked fear in the face and said, "Move over."

Change an Ordinary Routine in a Small Way

When your habits revolve around your comfort zone, they're anything but helpful. When we have the same old routine day after day, life starts to feel extremely dull. Counteract this by making one small change, even if it's too small it seems insignificant.

Do you go to the same coffee shop every morning? If so, go somewhere else. Do you make the same dinner or meal all the time? Then, find a new recipe and give that a try. What about your route to work? Is that always the same? Grab your GPS and look for a different route to get there. All of these things add up to create a significant effect because they snap you out of autopilot and let you really experience the world around you. Once you do, you'll realize what you've been missing by clinging to what's familiar.

Try One New Thing You've Always Wanted to Try

This ties into doing what scares you, but there's meant to be more of a reward attached to it. Most of us have list upon list detailing all the things we want to do, from skydiving to traveling the world. The sad part is, we never do any of these things because we're too busy 'living' (see: settling).

Take a pottery class. Go to Germany. Learn to SCUBA dive. Get a dog. Stop adding to that list—in fact, tear it up. Instead of writing something down for later, do it right then and there. If you wait for the time to be right, especially when you're still in your comfort zone, you'll never do it. There's no room for anything new within your self-imposed boundaries, so get out of them.

Say Yes to Something You've Said No to in the Past

Often, when we're in our comfort zone, our knee-jerk reaction is to say no. Saying no means that we're safe and that we don't run the risk of encountering an unfamiliar situation. This isn't always the case, of course. 'No' is sometimes necessary when we're genuinely concerned for our safety or feeling overburdened. However, the vast majority of the time, 'no' simply means "I'm afraid to say yes." Don't be afraid. Do it.

If a friend asks you to go to a ballroom dancing class, say yes.

If your kids ask you to take them to the park, but you have work to do, drop the work. Say yes. They'll only be young for so long.

When the barista asks if you want whipped cream on your coffee, definitely say yes.

It's not about mindlessly agreeing, it's about learning how 'yes' feels compared to 'no.' Saying yes to the little things is like saying yes to life.

Getting Comfortable Being Uncomfortable

I know I've spent a lot of time talking about changing the things in your life that you've felt comfortable with. When you decide to actively pursue your dreams, you have to do something that many of us struggle with. You have to get comfortable being uncomfortable.

What's that supposed to mean?

It means that being uncomfortable will become a fact of life as you continue to follow your dreams and push your limits. Once you get to a place where you feel comfortable with the changes you're going to make, you'll have to leave your comfort zone again.

The thing about pushing your limits and following your dreams is that it's an ongoing process. Human beings are adaptable. When we try something new, it's uncomfortable at first, but with the passage of time it becomes more comfortable. This often happens before we have reached our goals.

If you want to follow your dreams and actively pursue your vocation, you must be prepared to continue expanding your comfort zone.

Personal growth occurs outside your comfort zone.

So in order to continue to pursue your dreams, you must make the decision to feel comfortable with the discomfort. As soon as you decide that you are well with the discomfort, you will be able to leave your comfort zone much more easily.

This doesn't mean you don't feel uncomfortable. It just means you won't react negatively every time you do. You'll be prepared for it and better able to handle it.

I can speak from experience. It's not an easy thing to do, but it's extremely necessary. Pursuing your vocation or life purpose is a long-term effort.

Chapter 8 Self-Confidence and Self-Esteem – Two Things That Empaths Should Work Upon

Empaths are often found to struggle with self-confidence and self-esteem. They have a very low sense of worth. They rate themselves really low. And when these two qualities are present in low amounts, the empaths lose their balance. As you know, empaths are healers, and they expend their energy, trying to make others feel better. They forego the foundation of their own lives and do not take care of their own selves. Instead, they spend all their time and energy in assisting others. That is why they have low self-esteem and self-confidence in the first place.

The low levels of both these qualities are usually deeply rooted in the past and mostly in the childhood years of the person. It can be some form of trauma or emotional abuse. It can also be something like constant neglect from a parent, separation from parent figures, and sexual abuse. When you have low levels of self-esteem, you start seeing the world as this bad place where nothing good is possible. You automatically see everything in a hostile manner. And this is very commonly seen in empaths. This is also the reason why they miss out on so many interesting things in life, and they also feel that they cannot change things because they have become powerless. And this goes on and on like a vicious cycle lowering their self-esteem even further.

But if you want to break free from this downward spiral, then there is definitely a way out. There are several strategies that you can implement to enhance your self-confidence and boost your self-esteem. Here are some of them –

Practice Visualization

Visualization can help you in many ways when it comes to empowering yourself. In this technique, you have to see yourself as the person you want to be or the person you are proud of. This is because when people have low self-confidence, it is because they view themselves in a poor perception. This perception is not always accurate. But when you visualize yourself as the person you are trying to be, then you get an immediate bout of self-confidence. It might seem a bit daunting in the beginning, but with time, you will be able to improve your self-image.

You have to implement the strategies of creative visualization to achieve the results you want. It will identify all the negative beliefs that you have about yourself and then replace the same with positive ones. Yes, it will not happen in the span of a night, but you have to take the first step towards it and stay consistent if you want your efforts to bring fruitful results. Your aim should be protecting your subconscious from the negative thoughts and you also have to work on eliminating the toxic thoughts that are already present there.

So, your first task is to find a place where you can perform visualization. The place should be quiet and safe, and no one should disturb you there. You have to choose the place in such a way that you can be there for a period of time totally uninterrupted. You can also play some music that is relaxing or light some candles to create a soothing atmosphere. Then practice deep breathing for a few minutes as it will help you in eliminating the stress from your body. After that, close your eyes and start visualizing. You have to imagine yourself as this strong personality who does not get affected by petty negative matters in life. Your imagination cannot be vague; otherwise, it will not take effect. You have to be very specific about all the details you see.

No matter how busy you are, you should try to take out time on a daily basis and practice this exercise. If you can, then you can also do this twice a day for better results. You have to encourage yourself with motivational words and praise yourself. But you also have to remain patient. Remember that your negative self-image was not born in a day. It took you years to become like that, and so it is definitely going to take some time to undo that damage.

Create Positive Affirmations

When you utilize daily positive affirmations, it can really change the way you see your life. Affirmations are like these small positive statements that can keep you focused even when you are not, and they will help you overcome anything that comes your way.

Create your own positive affirmations that you will repeat throughout the day and keep them written in someplace and go through it right after you wake up in the morning. This will set you off in a good mood, and you will have the right vibe of energy in the morning. You have to believe in yourself that you can do it; otherwise, nothing is going to be possible.

Now, if you are wondering how you can create positive affirmations, here are some tips that you should keep in mind –

Always use first-person because that gives a certain empathic feel. Say 'I am' instead of anything else. This will sound really powerful.

You should always stay in the present tense while creating your affirmations.

You have to make it specific. You cannot be vague as to 'I will try to eliminate self-doubt.' You can say, 'I will not second guess my abilities in public speaking.'

You should keep these sentences in the positive. You have to affirm that you want something. The sentences should not be about what you don't want.

Try to include the –ing words because they indicate action.

Keep them concise and short. When you have a lesser number of words, your affirmations automatically become easier to recall. You can also try rhyming them.

You should center these affirmations around yourself. They should not be about someone else in your life.

There must be a 'feeling' word or some kind of dynamic emotion in your affirmation.

Once you have written down your affirmations, you have to make a promise to yourself that you are going to repeat them every day for at least five to ten minutes. I would always advise you to say them out loud because that exudes a high level of enthusiasm and energy.

Face Your Fears

If you want to increase your self-confidence levels, then you will have to come out of your comfort zone and face your fears. You have to remind yourself that self-confidence is nothing but a mindset that you have to acquire. Yes, you will feel powerless when you are afraid, but you also have to remember that you can take over your fears. Start by writing down your fears. Take a notebook and think about all those things that make you feel afraid. Once you have written them all down, now it is time to rank them according to the anxiety levels they cause.

Now, after you have ranked them, start from the bottom (the one that is least-anxiety inducing) and face them. You have to slowly work your way up the list. The first one that you try should not be too hard, and once you do it, you will automatically feel a boost in your self-confidence. Eventually, you will come to those fears which are of most importance in nature.

It is also important that you start rewarding yourself for every fear you face. This is because when you reward yourself, you automatically start attaching the feeling of overcoming fear with good feelings. The reward does not have to be anything elaborate. It can be something as simple as treating yourself to your favorite food, or it can also be watching your favorite TV series for a while. But one of the most important things about facing your fears is that you have to be honest with yourself. If you are not honest, then there will always be some fears that will stay suppressed. When you start meeting your fears head-on, every experience will give you newfound confidence.

Keep a Check on Your Inner Critic

Empaths often have an overactive inner critic and that is why they keep criticizing themselves more than necessary. If you think carefully, then you will notice that the harshest comment your receive on anything are usually from your own self. This not only lowers your confidence but also affects your self-esteem.

People are often so used to hearing their narrations that they do not really judge the messages that we are sending across to our subconscious. We tend to become oblivious to everything. You have to pay careful attention to whatever your thoughts are, and you need to remind yourself that not everything you think is true. Some thoughts can be biased and exaggerated.

You should also stop ruminating. Suppose you had a bad day at the office, and you kept rethinking all those moments over and over again which eventually led you to have a bad day at home too. When you keep on repeating the bad things in your head, you are actually making yourself feel worse. Also, there is a tendency in people that they start focusing on the same matter they are trying to avoid. So, the more you try to avoid something, the more you will be attracted to it. The solution lies in finding an alternative thought that you can stick to and this thought should be something positive.

You also have to learn when your thoughts are becoming too negative. In order to do so, gather all the evidence that you have in your possession and then examine them one by one. You will notice that the evidence will ultimately refute the prediction that you have made. If you are finding it difficult to gather the evidence to support your thoughts, writing them down in a piece of paper often helps. You have to be rational while you judge both sides of the argument.

Slowly, you have to learn to accept your flaws. Nobody is perfect, but instead of reminding yourself that you are not good at something, you can also try to encourage yourself to do better. When you accept your flaws or your weaknesses, it does not mean that they have to remain the way they are forever. You can always make progress if you want to.

Your inner critic has both positive and negative effects. It can either help you in achieving your full potential or it can completely ruin your chance of success. When you are too harsh on yourself with the self-talk, you are hindering your pace and reducing your chance to achieve your goals. So, when you tame your inner critic, it will help you know which areas require improvement, and then you can start on a more productive journey.

Stop Comparing Yourself to Others

Empaths have an identity that is very much vulnerable to the outside world, especially because of the fact that their self-esteem is not in good shape. They get easily affected by the energies of those around them. Whenever they are in some social gathering, they start comparing themselves to others. They start judging themselves on the basis that they are not good at something while others are. It can be the simplest thing in life but it can also be something complex.

But you have to realize the fact that you always try to focus on what you lack and not on what you have. When you continue to do this for an extended period of time, your brain becomes wired to disregard your own feelings and strengths. You take on a lot of stress than you can handle, and your performance is heavily affected because of this. What you have to do is learn to appreciate the skills that others possess. You need to stop seeing everyone in a way as if they are your competitors. Instead, you need to learn things from them by considering it as an opportunity to brush up on your skills. Your demeanor will undergo a lot of change the moment you change your perspective.

The human brain is meant to learn a lot of things when you do something on repeat, and that is why if you want this strategy to help you, you have to practice not comparing yourself to others whenever you are in a social place. When you keep doing this over and over again, it will become your second nature.

Stop Worrying About What Others Think

Empaths have this tendency to judge themselves based on what other people say or think. Their actions become totally biased. They cannot determine their personal value and always depend on others to do that for them. Also, in today's society with so much social media presence, it is pretty easy to get caught up with your outer appearance. So, you need to strengthen your thoughts and stop worrying. The social norms are the major reason why people worry about other people's perceptions of them. There is always something that is considered to be ideal, and whenever you deflect from the idealism, you start questioning yourself whether it is right or not. You fear that others will reject you or judge you. But you have to remind yourself that there is nothing wrong with you. The society has simply grown like this and it is responsible for inculcating this fear of judgment in everyone.

You have to learn to live in the moment and not worry about anything else. When you keep worrying about the smallest things in life, you lose confidence in your own self and suffer from low self-esteem. You cannot control everything in your life and so stop trying. Focus on who you are and ditch all the 'could' and 'if's because they are not your problem to worry about.

There is something else that you should consider. If you think carefully, you will notice how much we all are centered among ourselves and so is everyone around us. We might be thinking that others are constantly judging us or discussing something bad about us but that is not the case. People don't even care usually as they are concerned about their own problems just like you. Suppose when you are going out on a date, you might be thinking what others will think of your outfit but chances are that no matter what you wear, it will be the same to most people. Once you start to realize this, it will become easier.

Practice acceptance. You need to everything else at the bottom of your priority list and put yourself on top. You should be your biggest priority, and you should practice giving self-love at all times. You will learn about the various ways in which you can show self-love in a later part in this book. It will take you some time to get used to all of this but with a little bit of practice, everything shall fall in place.

Be around those who make you happy. You need to choose your friends carefully. Don't be with people who criticize you or make you feel bad about yourself. When someone truly cares about you, they will focus on your strengths and remind you what a good person you are. Also, when you feel judged, it really helps when you are in your group of friends, where you can discuss everything openly.

You also have to make yourself understand that no matter how hard you try, there will always be people in your life whom you cannot satisfy. No matter what you do, some people will always judge because that's the only thing they know. But those people should not really matter to you. Our life is too short to worry about such things and waste half of it. So, ditch all negative thoughts and enjoy your life to the fullest.

Chapter 9 Why is Self-Confidence Important?

Self-confidence is the fountainhead of everything else in your life. You draw from it to achieve and build the other areas of your life. Think of it as the fuel tank of your life. It's obviously not the physical fuel; it's not something that you can reduce to a substance, but nonetheless, it exists. People might not realize this but self-confidence gives you power to achieve in all areas of your life.

Career

Self-confidence is important for your career because, like it or not, businesses are looking for leaders. When you check out that want ad, and you see that they're looking for an entry-level person, you can bet that if you are a person who positions himself or herself as a future leader, you will go places in that company. It doesn't matter whether you applied for a seemingly dead-end job; once the business enterprise sees you as potential leader material, they would invest in you. They would have a vested interest in your personal development. You have to understand that businesses live or die based on how effectively they can turn rank and file employees into leaders.

Now, this leadership position can take a wide variety of shapes. You can be a frontline leader, meaning like you can be a low-level manager. You can be a member of the middle management, or you can become a vice-president or even CEO. It all really depends on you.

What's important to understand here is that businesses are desperate for future leaders because, let's face it, the vast majority of people who apply for jobs do so because they just need to pay the rent. They're just looking to making ends meet. They're not looking at the future; they're looking at their short-term needs and, accordingly, most of them never become leaders. It's completely outside of their conception of their place in the company. They're just looking to solve a problem.

If you're a confident person, you can become a leader. You can project an air that things can be done. You can inspire others, not only with your productivity, but with the emotional signals that you send out. People become optimistic around you. You can boost productivity simply because you inspire people.

These are the types of individuals businesses are looking to develop and promote, because if they are able to produce enough leaders, they will blow away their competition. Why? Their competition is staffed by people who have very short-term attitudes. Those people are simply looking to do a day's work for a day's pay. Nothing more, nothing less. A company staffed almost 100% of people with that mentality isn't going far. It will always be beaten by companies that have leaders. However, for you to become a leader, you have to have self-confidence.

Relationships

Relationships involve two different people, two different egos, two different backgrounds, and two different pasts. Whenever there is difference, it can be a very exciting thing because, let's face it, there's nothing more exciting than talking and dealing with somebody who experienced things that are very different from yours.

Now, as amazing as this difference may be, it also leads to conflict, because you didn't come from the same place. You didn't experience the same things; you didn't have the same ideas and influences growing up. Accordingly, when you're in a relationship, it's too easy to look at it as competition. It's too easy to look at it as somebody winning and somebody losing.

Unfortunately, if you have low self-confidence, it's very easy for you to gravitate towards an attitude where you believe that it's better not to assert yourself and your needs lest the other person might leave. In other words, you let your fear of losing them take over your relationship. It's no longer a relationship at that point.

You have to remember that relationships are spaces and arrangements that let both people grow. It's very hard to grow when you're always denying yourself. It's very hard to truly blossom when you feel like you have to hold yourself in because you're afraid that you would lose the other person in the relationship. Ultimately, without self-confidence your identity in the relationship becomes subsumed into the identity of your partner. In other words, the relationship is all about them, their needs, their plans, their future, and you then are left making all sorts of excuses as to why you let this happen.

One common excuse is to simply fool yourself into thinking that you're doing everything that you could do to support the relationship. You're not supporting the relationship because you're completely out of it. The relationship is not your partner. Unfortunately, that's when your support takes the form of denying yourself and your needs and your identity within the relationship. All you're managing to do is support your partner and nobody else.

You need to be strong in your conviction to keep on loving. You need to carve out your own identity. You need to make sure that your relationship is built on a solid foundation of respect and equality. None of these are possible if you don't have self-confidence.

For your relationship to be healthy, you have to get noticed. The other partner must not only notice you but give you proper respect and take your feedback. Furthermore, they must defer to you from time to time. In other words, you need to make your voice felt. This is almost impossible to do without self-confidence.

Another reason why self-confidence helps you in your relationship is because, let's face it, there's no such thing as a perfect relationship. People can and do screw up. Your partner or you can be unfaithful. You can say the wrong things at the wrong time and hurt each other. All sorts of things can go wrong.

Given all this, it's important to persevere. It's important to bounce back in a relationship. Make no mistake about it, your partner can say something so crushing, so cutting and so humiliating that it's very easy for you to throw in the towel and just walk out. However, you don't. If the relationship is worth it, you don't. You hang in there. It requires resilience. You need to hang in there long enough for you to communicate in such a way that he or she learns from that sad experience and gives you proper respect. That's not going to happen if you don't have enough self-confidence going in.

It's too easy for your relationship to become so fragile based on such low self-esteem that its only a matter of time until either of you walks away. If you think this is difficult enough, understand that getting into a relationship in the first place requires confidence. Why? You need to stand out from other suitors.

If your partner is very attractive or appealing, you can bet that there would be other suitors. It depends on their level of appeal. Of course, the more attractive or appealing the partner, the more competition you have. However, even if your partner is not all that attractive, there's still at least one person that is interested in your partner, or your partner might be interested in somebody else. To stand out from the competition, you need self-confidence. At the very least, you should be able to make a case for yourself as to why your prospective partner should pick you instead of somebody else.

Life Enjoyment

In terms of quality of life, self-confidence is crucial. You start believing that you really don't matter all that much. You start believing that you really can't speak up because your voice doesn't really count for anything.

You can't live life without speaking out for your needs. Why? People can and will step on you. You see, life is a dog-eat-dog landscape; it really is. Forget everything that you've heard before. It's not a world of sunshine, smiles, unicorns and lollipops. It can be brutal out there. Unfortunately, far too many people move in when they detect any kind of weakness. If you give somebody an inch, it's not uncommon for them to want to take a mile. If you give somebody a hand, don't be surprised if they want to take your arm as well.

You have to be able to speak up for your needs. You have to be able to stand on your rights. You can't just live in the shadows and constantly give in. It's going to get in the way of your enjoyment of your life. You feel you're simply settling for something that is getting smaller and smaller with each passing day. You start feeling that you are a bystander in your life, and regardless of how you feel, and regardless of what's going on, and how hurt you become, it really doesn't really matter all that much because you don't matter all that much. You see how corrosive this is? You understand how you have set up yourself to live such a pathetic life? It is pathetic because you are capable of so much more.

The bottom line is if you want to be successful in anything, you have to be confident in yourself. Nobody can do it for you. Nobody else would do it for you. Nobody else can do it for you.

Chapter 10 How to motivate yourself?

We all want to achieve something, so we set up a goal and try to accomplish it. But you would surely accept that setting up a goal is one thing but turning that goal into reality is completely different and a hard process. We often set a million goals to fulfill, but at the end of the month, most of the goals are become abandoned by a precious number of people. When we set a goal, we often tend to get dreamy about it. We sit back and get us into the fantasy land, where we dream ourselves as winners, with all of our goals accomplished. But after some days of the initial enthusiasm, we forget to light up that fire inside ourselves.

If you really want to be a successful person, you must keep the fire lit within yourself. To stay motivated, you must need some outside stimuli. That's why we're offering you some ways to help you do that.

Write down the reasons behind your claim.

As you list down your goals, write a few reasons why do you want to accomplish it. This will give you a fair purpose not to give up. Name those things you will be able to do after accomplishing your goals that will give you some inspirations and will energize you. This will also help you to track the progress of your journey. This is very important for people to be aware of why they have been performing the tasks.

Give yourself a reason to smile

Smile is the best remedy of all sorts of negative impacts that we have in our life. So, whatever happens to ourselves we must not give up the habit of smiling that keeps us alive even at the darkest hour of our life. This concept is also applicable in this case of gaining motivation to focus indomitably on your goals. Though we have many negative issues to deal with in our daily life but there are a lot of reasons too for making ourselves refreshed from the dilemma of internal and external affairs. Here the smile acts as the mentor of those small but everlasting memories that opens an affirmative doorway for us in the world surrounded by downwards conceptions and chaotic mentality created by conventional maintainers.

To keep your smile fresh and active you must follow some healthy habits that are both philosophically and socially very wealthy. First of all, you have to found always the positive sparks not only in the outer world but also within yourself that always gives you to be one step ahead from where you generally belong to. It is only possible when you make your mind free to deal with any kind of situation in your daily life. When you become habituated by that kind of activities, you become also a person to keep yourself positive through the appearance of a smile in your face.

Secondly, don't take the pressure to make others happy through your personal choices. Your personal choices are mainly built up to refresh your mental situation apart from outward belongings. So, if it is combined with outward, it is spoilt, and moreover, the people would interfere in your own world, and it will make a negative impact on your mind.

According to the need of globalization, one must follow some attitude to deal with this particular era. One of them is diplomacy. You must be diplomatic to make yourself perfect to the outer world and on this occasion, you should always think positive about anyone you meet. But don't let them understand your drawbacks.

Maintain your grass-root beginning

It is no doubt that success is the most preferable option of life that is inhabitable and the way of this ultimate goal is not comfortable so much. It is like a staircase where you have to achieve the sky view through one by one step. So, you have to start with an impression of learning from experiences. It will make you confident about yourself because in this process there will no gap exist in your way to achieve the goals. Always think yourself as a learner and keep yourself ready to enjoy new experiences.

Judge yourself first.

A mistake is a part of your activity as we all know- "Failure is a pillar of success". So, it is very essential to identify your mistakes, learn from them and rectify them as soon as possible.

But here, one thing keeps our road blocked. That is the way of judging, not of oneself but the others. It is a very negative attitude in the field of application. Sometimes it makes you to give lame excuses against your fault and complaining about others and make them responsible for the act. So you should change this attitude. You must judge yourself first, and make yourself eligible by collecting them with your sincerity and attentive behavior. It will also help you to focus on yourself. Otherwise, your motivation would be diverted and it will be harder to achieve your dreaming goals.

It is also a public relationship motto that we should always maintain in every field of our life. When you judge others and cover your false with lame excuses, it spoils your social relationships and affects your co-operative surroundings. The consequence of this act will make you suffer from helplessness during the time of vital assistance. So, always find your own fault by examining own attitude and behavior and make it perfect and more acceptable to the people you surrounded by.

Overcome your fear

Each and every moment we have to step forward to make our life affirmative and successful. But it is not an easy process. There are many obstacles found in this way of success. Some of them belong to the external world which can be ignored or solved by our attitude, determination and liabilities. But some of them make their residence within our sense. These are more harmful than the former, because we have to fight with them without any external support. One of them is – 'Fear'. Though the word is very small to hear but it is one of the most harmful terms that make us inactive and downward throughout our life. Fear cannot be objectified. We can only feel it according to our situation. Though it is an abstract object but in our practical life, it decreases our determination and makes us think from a negative corner even at the door of our success.

Fear can be categorized into many parts. One thing is clear. Whatever the fear is, we have to fight against it all alone. Sometimes we can share our situations with the dearest ones. It will give you an assurance that fear is not the only element that exists within yourself. So, during the investigation, you should also find out your positive skills that will definitely defeat your fears and make you think affirmative about yourselves.

Chapter 11 The Art of Self Love

Why Should We Love Ourselves the Right Way?

Self-love has grown into one of the most popular buzzwords in the self-improvement department — and it's for a good reason. These days, experts and ordinary people alike are quickly learning about the importance of loving oneself first in order to become the kind of people that they aspire to be. This makes a lot of sense, because after all, it is only in prioritizing our own well-being do we make it easier for ourselves to accept opportunities and face adversities.

What Self-Love is NOT

Before we talk about the importance of cultivating self-love on a daily basis, we must first briefly dissect what self-love is NOT. See, some people may have an aversion to the concept of self-love because they think that it's uncomfortably all about the self — "me, myself, and I". However, that could not be further from the truth.

Just because the "self" is placed before "love", it doesn't mean that you're free to do whatever you want without any regard for how it will affect the people around you. It's more about caring for yourself in a way that makes you function optimally —

without taking anything away from others. Hence, self-love is not equivalent to:

• Selfishness

• Egotistical behaviors

• Arrogance

• Entitlement

• Total indifference to other people's thoughts and feelings

While individuals who exhibit the aforementioned traits may indeed "love themselves" — perhaps, a tad bit too much — that's obviously not the kind of "self-love" that we're trying to promote in this book. This kind of "love" — if we can even call it that — revolves around selfish people's fixation in filling a void within themselves. It's fueled by their preoccupation to find ways to constantly feed their egos.

What Self-Love IS

The real value of self-love lies in being at peace with yourself. It's all about treating your own happiness and well-being with utmost importance. It eliminates the need to sacrifice parts of who you really are to get others to see you and admire you. No, it doesn't mean that you're putting yourself on a pedestal, standing high above others.

Self-love simply encourages you to accept yourself in your entirety — strengths, flaws, achievements, downfalls. You learn to understand that all those things — even if some of them aren't exactly beautiful, are just parts of who you are.

More importantly, self-love isn't a free pass to give in to instant gratification. Oftentimes, people think that rewarding themselves in the moment is an act of self-love, but those feelings of happiness are usually fleeting. Self-love is more about giving your mind, body, and soul the nourishment it needs to sustain you for the long haul. It's never about chasing earthly pleasures that only feel good right now. Self-love is learning how to give yourself the necessary care and attention that will protect your inner peace for the rest of your life.

Yes, loving yourself is important, but it's more important that you love yourself the right way. This book will share with you some habits that can help you do just that.

Silence Your Critical Inner Voice

All of us, in at least one point in our lives, have heard those voices in our heads that insist that we're not good enough. While it's important to rightfully accept that there were moments when we weren't at our best, regularly beating ourselves up for our shortcomings also doesn't do anything to help us. When we always let that critical inner voice take over our minds, it becomes easier for us to believe everything it says is true, and that nothing good can ever come out of us.

Destructive Criticism vs. Constructive Criticism

Giving too much power to your critical inner voice prevents you from learning to properly love not just yourself, but also those around you. When you become used to thinking that nothing about you is good, it will readily translate to how you perceive others. And, if you're truly being honest with yourself, being hypercritical hasn't really gotten you that far in life.

Yes, you might have achieved a fair amount of success because you nitpick everything that comes your way. But the real question is: are you happy — in the truest sense of the word?

Hence, it's important that you learn to distinguish between the good kind of criticism (constructive) versus the bad kind (destructive). Undeniably, there will always be areas in our lives that are ripe for improvement. However, it's important that we assess them in a constructive way — asking questions that focus on what happened, and not on how wrong we were.

Constructive criticisms inspire us to change for the better. Destructive criticisms, on the other hand, only aim to break us apart. Self-love all starts with clearing our minds with hyper-negative thoughts about ourselves.

Be Gentler with Yourself

How you love yourself is how you teach others to love you.

-       Rupi Kaur

Oftentimes, people find it a lot easier to be gentler and more considerate to their family and friends than to themselves. This is generally a result of having to live with a hypercritical inner voice for most of their lives. Being fed with judgmental thoughts — by none other than yourself — can leave you feeling ashamed of what you're really feeling. As a result, these feelings that you can't express are left to rot inside of you — often causing a massive stench that eventually becomes difficult to hide.

Gentleness as the Antithesis of Shame

Unfortunately, most of us have been taught from an early age that feelings — particularly the negative kinds — are nothing more than a nuisance. Hence, it's quite normal for us to associate "having feelings" with "weakness". The thing is, we can't proceed with self-love if we continue to demonize feelings — something that naturally comes with our humanity.

Learning how to be gentle with yourself is the first step towards overcoming the shame that surrounds your true emotions. This is why it's essential to practice taming your critical inner voice. This voice will try to drown out the things that you really need to hear, thereby preventing you from facing the real gravity of what's really bothering you.

Instead of fighting with yourself, or thinking of ways to change or fix "what's wrong" with you, those feelings of shame will have a better chance of going away if you start being gentler with yourself and what you're dealing with. You don't have to let negativity and judgments overwhelm you. If you could learn how to sit with your own feelings like you would keep a child company, then you'd have a better chance of finding inner peace.

Take Care of Your Mind and Body

Your job is to fill your cup, so it overflows. Then, you can serve others, joyfully from your saucer.

- Lisa Nichols

Procrastination is often caused by hypercritical minds that are obsessed with perfect results. See, when people are too focused on the end product, it can hold them back from doing what they have to do. This leads them to doubt themselves and the entire process — only to realize that their deadline is already drawing near.

As a result, they get too overwhelmed, and they begin to work twice as hard to make up for all the time they wasted on being critical. Thus, they pull off all-nighters, skip meals, flake on their friends, and beat themselves to the pulp — basically forgetting about their overall health just to accomplish everything on time. But what does that have to do with self-love?

Love Comes Easy When You Feel Your Best

Ignoring one's health is the perfect invitation for all sorts of stress. And stress, when it becomes a constant entity in your life, can be the spark that ignites mental health issues like depression and anxiety. As you may already know, a mind that can't function well will lead to a body that breaks and a heart that forgets how to properly process emotions.

Yes, putting in the work is important, but you won't be able to produce the great stuff if your mind and body are falling apart. You simply can`t pour from an empty cup. This also makes it incredibly difficult for you to see what's worth loving about life and yourself. On the other hand, if you put in the effort to feel your best every day, you'll make it a lot easier to stay consistent with your new self-love practices.

Learn How to be Comfortable with Yourself

People who constantly subject themselves to endless cycles of self-judgments are often unhappy with the way they are. It could be because they associate certain aspects of themselves to things that they have aversions for. Obviously, this will only brew extreme feelings of discontent with themselves — something that not even a "new identity" can resolve. After all, the "broken parts" will never really go away.

Growing Into Who You Really Are

Such discomfort with oneself is one of the biggest hurdles to learning about self-love. That's because you keep on chasing the person that you're not, and keep on rejecting the person that you really are. You are hiding the real you, even from yourself. And when you keep this real you hidden, it would be impossible to completely love you for you.

Yes, feeling accepted is necessary for us to be happy in life. But acceptance needs to come from you first and foremost. You can't ever fully love yourself and the life you're given if you're busy grooming yourself to be accepted by others first. And if you're like this, chances are, you may also have unwarranted expectations of others, which just forces both of you to live inauthentic and dissatisfying lives.

Hence, it's necessary to get to know who you are deep inside, even if you're utterly flawed. These imperfections are what make you unique, after all. It is only in this way that you get to accept that you'll forever be a work in progress — always making mistakes, but always growing nonetheless. This is the path to finding comfort in oneself, and ultimately finding self-love.

Do Not Compare Yourself to Others

If you judge a fish by its ability to climb a tree, it will live its whole life believing it is stupid.

-        Albert Einstein

A fish doesn`t have to climb a tree nor a monkey has to run as fast as a horse. You will master self-love when you stop comparing your lows with someone`s else highs. True self-love is only possible when you focus on becoming a better you. There's a reason why "envy" is considered by Christianity as one of the Seven Deadly Sins, or why people created the saying, "Comparison is the thief of joy". That's because having unhealthy desires for what we don't have is often the seed that grows a forest of negative self-talk. When you always look at others and think about how great they are compared to you, you'll end up with thoughts like:

•   "I'm not good enough for this."

•   "There's just nothing that I can do right."

•   "I'll never amount to anything."

Your Life is Your Own to Live

Oftentimes, it's necessary for us to look up to others or to find role models so we can work on living the life that we want. However, there's a tendency for us to be hard on ourselves when we put in the effort and still, we aren't anything like them. This is why comparison isn't anything worthwhile, and will only stall your self-love journey.

Constant comparison only leads us to struggle with more insecurities. Besides, we shouldn't even be comparing ourselves to people while they're already at their top. We are seeing their results, and what we're dealing with now is just the behind-the-scenes. Of course, the end product is always going to look good when you compare it to the process!

The people you look up to live their lives the way they should have — by pursuing their passions and by focusing on what they can do to fulfill their dreams. They got things done because they spend little time looking at how others are doing. The sooner you find peace with the fact that there's always bound to be someone better than you at a particular area, the easier it will be for you to live your own life to the fullest and forget about theirs.

Accept Your Feelings for What They Really Are

When you accept your feelings without judgement, you give them permission to melt away.

-        Unknown

As we discussed in Lesson #2, hypercritical people usually have a hard time being gentle with themselves. This manifests in having a lot of bottled up feelings — ones that have been cast aside to avoid the shame that surrounds them. While this may help people feel strong in the moment, in the end, this is merely a form of escaping reality.

Acknowledging the Full Range of Your Emotions

Emotions are part of being human; there is simply no way around that. We don't have an internal switch that we can just turn off to avoid negative feelings — or turn on to feel the positive ones. If you've always had an aversion for feelings, this whole idea of "accepting" them might be something that you're battling with. After all, why would you even want to feel something that is as bad as you think it is?

However, it's worth noting that the more that you keep your feelings at bay, the wilder they become in the long run. And when they don't burst out in the form of uncontrolled anger, they often come out through destructive behaviors like drinking alcohol or taking drugs. This happens as a way of numbing the pain or forgetting about it temporarily.

In order to truly understand how self-love works, it's important for us to acknowledge that we have a full range of emotions. In so doing, we'll eventually develop the capacity to feel them in all of their weights and colors.

See, choosing only to feel the good stuff and casting aside pain and anger actually leads to more suffering. That's because it throws us into this endless cycle of shaming and judging ourselves. On the other hand, when we let ourselves feel things as they really are, it becomes easier for us to accept ourselves and the experiences that shape us.

Start Writing on a Journal

It is better to light a small candle than to curse the darkness.

-       Confucius

The self-love journey is often a fascinating one, but it's difficult to gauge how far you've really come when you have nothing tangible to look back on. Don't you just love it when you can see how much you've progressed? Additionally, the process will involve a lot of conflicting feelings that can be hard to deal with if you just keep them inside your mind. For these scenarios, the best solution is to write down your thoughts and feelings to gain some clarity (there is a super bonus at the end of this course that will help you to do just that).

Writing Reveals What You Need to Focus On

Oftentimes, it's hard for people to fully understand what's going on in their lives until they see how it looks outside of their heads. Take, for instance, how it's usually easier for people to listen to their friends' issues and give solicited advice than to solve their own issues.

This can be utterly frustrating when you feel like you're always hitting a dead end when you're on your own. To get past this hurdle, you can start putting your problems on a piece of paper so you can "physically" see it. This usually does a couple of things. First, writing down what's bothering you allows you to process the problem in a whole new way. That's because your mind and body are both engaged in it. This usually paves the way towards acceptance.

 Second, recording it through writing makes it easier to start your healing process. That's because you're literally facing your problems on the page — you're not escaping them this time. Your journal will hold the truest parts of you in your most vulnerable moments. It's only in seeing these versions of yourself will you learn the value of knowing and loving yourself for real.

Conclusion

As you have been able to see through the various chapters of this book, self-esteem is a very complex and very in-depth thing to address. Everyone is so different and we all have such different upbringings that is hard to pinpoint a generic way someone should be raised to avoid self-esteem issues. And while we'll never really figure out this universal way to raise someone, we have been able to figure out ways to combat the effects of low self-esteem, as well as how to build up someone's self-esteem.

As you've been able to see through this book, being confident in yourself is one of the greatest gifts you can have. The more confident you are with your decisions and yourself as a human being, the better your life will be.

And while everything might have seemed really overwhelming as you read through the book, it's important that you remember that you were taking the very first steps to changing who you are as a person. As mentioned at the very beginning of this book, changing yourself and doing a complete overhaul of who you are is one of the hardest and most daunting tasks anyone can do. It takes dedication and sacrifice to open a book such as this one and commit yourself to it and to use it to change yourself as a person.

Always remember that, no matter what, you can always change your situation for the better. We often get too caught up in the intricacies of his complex society we live in that we forget to bring it down to the basics and worry about ourselves first. Life is very short and, before you know it, you're going to be sitting there in old age while looking back at your life and thinking about all the regrets and great times that you had. It's important to remember that while you're still young, there's a lot you can change. Go out there and change your life and become the best version of you possible because, when you're 80 years old and looking back, you want to look at this moment in time and say to yourself, "Damn, that was the best time of my life".

CPSIA information can be obtained
at www.ICGtesting.com
Printed in the USA
BVHW041746201120
593806BV00011B/697